T0168078

Postal

Postal

Brock Wilbur &
Nathan Rabin

Boss Fight Books
Los Angeles, CA
bossfightbooks.com

ISBN 13: 978-1-940535-22-7
First Printing: 2020

Series Editor: Gabe Durham
Associate Editor: Michael P. Williams
Book Design by Cory Schmitz
Page Design by Christopher Moyer and Lori Colbeck

For Vivian,
who willingly agreed to be complicit in
[gestures wildly] this whole mess

— Brock Wilbur

To my furry little bastard, Ghostface

— Nathan Rabin

I've done a lot of foolish things
that I really didn't mean
I could be a broken man but here I am
with your future, got your future babe
Here I am baby
Signed, sealed, delivered

— Stevie Wonder, 1970

CONTENTS

PART I

POSTAL: THE VIDEO GAME

BY BROCK WILBUR

SLEEPOVER

My homeschooled friend let me know that he wasn't allowed to play *Super Mario Bros.* because of the violence.

I'll say that again, so that it might emulate the one-two punch I felt at twelve years of age: Sweet, colorful, silly *Super Mario Bros.* was too violent to be allowed in his home. It is the first moment I can remember in my formative years of hearing the opinion of another human being and wholly rejecting it. Not just on a conversational level, but equally on a physical and mayhaps metaphysical level. A darkness twitched within me, and a torrent of word-sounds poured out onto an unsuspecting victim whose only crime was revealing a single detail of his home life. And for that, I would nearly destroy him.

Matthew was homeschooled because we were growing up in central Kansas and Matthew's father was a preacher. Matthew was older than me, but he couldn't be trusted to attend public school, where demonic vice-principals might awkwardly inform him about the existence of sex before marriage or explain how to cover a banana with a condom. Our lives had only intersected because the town's community theater had a summer musical production for idiot kids who weren't cool enough to know that no one needed another staging of *Godspell* in central Kansas. Jesus was already cool enough around the metropolis of Salina.

An aside for context: The next year, Matthew (and the rest of the homeschooled kids) wouldn't be allowed to show up for a production of *Once Upon a Mattress* due to its overly sexual themes—namely, mattresses. I never saw him again. Through mutual friends, I heard that when Matthew came of age to get a driver's license, he was required to recite a book of the Bible, in its entirety, from memory before his family would let him head to the DMV. He successfully delivered 1 Corinthians in its entirety but failed the driving test. I can't confirm any of this, but it seems too on-brand to be anything less than true.

Anyway.

Matthew wasn't allowed to play *Super Mario Bros.* This wasn't 1985, when the game came out. This was in 1997. Marilyn Manson existed. *Event Horizon* was in theaters. I had been shooting dudes in the dick in *GoldenEye 007* for several weeks. In that cultural landscape, how do you wrap your mind around a kid two years your senior living sheltered from the horror of an 8-bit mustachioed Italian man sliding down tubes and collecting coins? Not only did Matthew share this information with me, he defended his family's decision to protect him from such vile trash.

Hilariously, Matthew's family wasn't that far away from mine on the conservative spectrum. My father wrote opinion pieces for the local paper, advocating for parents to shield their children from corrosive and dangerous programming such as *Ren & Stimpy*, *Beavis and Butt-Head*, and the Gremlins films. Even *The Simpsons* was off-limits. When I showed up to grade school the morning of these op-eds, I was predictably bullied by the cooler kids, and just like Matthew I took my dad's side. "*Beavis and Butt-Head* makes you stupid," I would declare. I didn't know what I was missing, so it was easy to take my dad's side until one night at a friend's house when I saw two episodes of *Ren & Stimpy* and the bonkers third act of *Gremlins 2*. Basking in the manic joy of forbidden media, I realized my dad—and maybe all adults—were just weird killjoys for no reason. It was time to circumnavigate the world of rules. The world of bullshit adult rules.

I resolved to save Matthew from his fate. He was a Rod & Todd of the highest order, but certainly the saved Christian boy could be saved again by the power of dangerous pop culture. So I invited Matthew to a sleepover. Teenage boy sleepovers are traditionally a source of salvation through experimentation, and boy howdy did I have a plan.

The local pre-Blockbuster rental store was a mom-and-pop operation that opened a video game section one Friday by simply placing a large number of PC games in boxes along a wall. These floppy discs and CD-ROMs were in no way meant to be legally rented out, and I suspect the kindly folks running this shop had little idea of what the plain brown package with the word "POSTAL" contained—or else their good Christian morals would certainly not have allowed them to place it on a shelf next to a title as wholesome-seeming as *SimCity*. I didn't know anything about the game, but I knew it was a bit of the ole Danger-Bad that I needed to experience. Sure, the rating on the cover should've warned attentive parents that this game was off-limits, but who knew what a context-free capital M meant unless they leaned in close enough to read the tiny "MATURE" above it?

That night, Matthew came to the Wilbur house, and immediately I wanted to share with him the gospel of gore and adults-only entertainment. Unfortunately, it took nearly thirty minutes to get the game installed and configured on our Gateway 2000 personal computer.

As the software installed, we passed the time reading the text on the back of the *Postal* box:

Welcome to Paradise… Arizona. They're out to get you (or are they?) It doesn't matter, you don't have time to think, only time to kill. GO POSTAL!! Blast, maim and fire-bomb your way through 17 unsuspecting locales from a small town to a heavily guarded military complex… Conspiracy or Insanity? Don't get too crazy - this killing spree is anything but senseless. Out here, strategy is key - and the locals are packin' - so take advantage of the third-person "premeditated" perspective that lets you see exactly who's cold and who's still able to pull a trigger. […] So freakin' real, your victims actually beg for mercy and scream for their lives! Real-time 3D characters rage against beautifully hand-painted killing fields. […] Mass Murder opportunities: spray protesters, mow down marching bands, and char-broil whole towns.

Wow. So edge, such cool. But for a twelve-year-old Midwestern kid who wasn't allowed to watch R-rated movies, this was like getting your first boner. I'd deceived a series of grown-ups into making this happen, and this poor preacher's kid was about to be born again in my unholy image.

I made Matthew sit next to me as the game loaded up.

"Oh man, just you wait," I said. "You're going to love this."

The game opened with a screen that said "Fair Warning: You Must Be 17 Or Older To Play."

Matthew, recognizing that this applied to neither of us, began to squirm. In my memory, I grabbed his hand to keep him in the chair, but to be fair that could just be the homoerotic subtext of what was going down.

Then the game began. A man with a gun appeared on screen in a small town, and he was mine to control. A bunch of cops started shooting at him so I opened fire on them. Once they were dead, I shot a bunch of townsfolk. All my victims screamed, and one of them exploded. Then someone I couldn't see shot me and I died. Yet another schizophrenic man executed by the police in America, a clear example of the systemic—Oh, Matthew is gone.

Matthew was on the ground holding his stomach. "I'm very sick and I think I need to go home. Would you call my dad?"

I called his family, and in the eight minutes before they arrived I attempted to deliver Matthew some last-ditch salvation by explaining to him the plot and murders of the film *Se7en*, even though I hadn't seen it and had only pieced together five of the deaths from things I heard from older high schoolers. This did not help his condition, so he locked himself in the bathroom until his dad arrived.

I didn't save Matthew. But I did render a kid violently ill with video game mayhem in under thirty seconds. Once you've seen power like that firsthand, it's hard not to spend the rest of your life fixating on the machinations of these dark arts.

That was the last time I would play *Postal* until Nathan and I started to work on this book in 2015. But its corrosive power over Matthew stayed with me for years.

It's hilarious that this power would come from a dumb game like *Postal*. It wasn't the best or most interesting violent video game. It wasn't even one of the most popular. This situation is comparable to a weird Christian kid who hears his first rock 'n' roll song, and it scares him so much that he comes to worship that song—even though that song is performed by Limp Bizkit. Which maybe that happened to me too. Fuck off. You didn't 1997 the way I 1997'd. You gotta have Faith.

THE BALLS TO
MAKE A GAME SO
FUNNY AND MEAN

POSTAL WAS THE 1997 DEBUT game by Running With Scissors (RWS), a small company of game industry vets based in Tucson, Arizona, who'd made some games for kids and wanted to strike out for more "mature" territory. A *Wall Street Journal* headline memorably called theirs a transition "from Miss Piggy to 'Kill the Pigs.'"

It was one of those games that generated plenty of buzz among players before it was even out. The free demo version of *Postal* was the most-downloaded demo for nearly a month on Happy Puppy—at the time one of the biggest game sites on the internet.

When *Postal* came out, the news media was at peak Videogame Fearmongering—but this was back when the conversation had more earnestness to it. While today's politicians blame video games for the world's ills merely because the NRA tells them to, in the 90s our culture's Fear of Games was rooted in the Fear of the New. Maybe games were fine, or maybe they existed to lure Dungeons & Dragons sorcerers into the woods for blood séances. (It did alarm parents to hear their kids casually use words like "stamina" and "scimitar.") Inside the space of this unsolved mystery, *Postal* thrived. Just for being more violent and having a less virtuous protagonist than the competition, the game developed a cachet it hadn't earned.

1997 was also when the anti-obscenity activist and yet-to-be-disbarred attorney Jack Thompson was turning his attention from rap music to video games. After the Heath High School shooting in December of that year, he represented the families of three victims in suing the makers of violent games that the shooter had played, such as *Doom*, *Mechwarrior*, and *Resident Evil*. While the lawsuit was thrown out, gamers wondered which of their favorite violent and obscene games might be next.

Postal met resistance elsewhere. Walmart banned the game. ("You can't buy Postal at Walmart, but you can buy a real gun," Desi noted.) RWS received plenty of hate mail. Most memorably, the local American Postal Workers Union boycotted the game, and union local president Mo Merow said in a statement that the game "humiliates the entire postal workforce." They later scaled back when they realized their tactics had unintended effects. "That sparked new interest in the game, sort of defeating the purpose of what the union was trying to do," said an unnamed United States Postal Service (USPS) representative to the *Philadelphia Inquirer*'s John J. Fried.

Merow and his union gave the game way too much credit. It's not even about a postal worker—it's just using the phrase in the casual sense to mean "a guy who's gone crazy." That didn't stop the USPS from suing RWS founder Vince Desi for its use of the word "postal," which they claimed was proprietary. Desi also reported that his company fielded concerned calls from both the FBI and the Treasury Department.

The game got so much more press than other games of its size and quality. "Something for the whole (Manson) family," wrote the *Washington Post*. Even in the moralizing articles condemning the game, it often sounded as if the journalist was having fun.

The media also made comparisons between *Postal* and the 1993 movie *Falling Down*, in which an everyman office drone played by Michael Douglas goes on a killing spree. While at the time of its release *Falling Down* got a pass as dark satire about the many stressors of modern life, today it reads more as a Trumpian white rage entitlement fantasy.

Postal, a small-screen product with no star power and an idiotic premise, felt the full brunt of the typical hand-wringers. Senator Joe Lieberman spoke out against the game: "This is sick stuff, and sadly it sells," he said, calling *Postal* (and *Carmageddon*, a racing game that encourages running over pedestrians) "digital poison."

Publisher Ripcord leaned into the controversy, promoting *Postal* to potential customers as "a dark, addictive and totally innovative psychological thriller so blatantly brutal, so sickeningly psychotic, victims actually scream for their lives, and pile up like waste during a big city garbage strike." After the demo version sparked outcry in Europe and Australia, an alternate version of *Postal* was created for international audiences in which women no longer scream "I can't breathe" or "Just kill me now," the game's tasteless ending is changed, and the infamous marching band sequence is removed. Even with this new, "toned-down" version, Australia's Office of Film and Literature Classification prohibited the game's release.

The American gaming press was less squeamish about the blood but harder on the faulty mechanics. GameSpot gave it a 6.6/10, AllGame gave it 3/5 stars, and Game Revolution gave it a B-.

Despite the middling reviews, the game was kept afloat in the cultural consciousness not just by its blatant shock value, but by the extreme reactions it provoked from perennially offended news outlets and opportunistic politicians. Even years later, it remains a topic of note in the history of violent video games.

"The game succeeded in part because the violence is accompanied by a perverse sort of humor; the story lines hold a dirty mirror up to America and make fun of everyone, regardless of their race, sex or ethnicity," the *Washington Post* wrote very generously about the game in 2005.

For fans, it didn't matter that *Postal* kinda sucked to play. It was a symbolic victory, an envelope-pusher. "I think this game is kick ass," says a commenter on Metacritic. "Why? Because nobody else has the balls to make a game so funny and mean…"

Postal was the garbage darling of the season.

WELCOME TO PARADISE

THE GAME OPENS WITH NO FANFARE. Nor does it hint at what will come next or offer instructions as to what any of the buttons on your keyboard do.

Your character, a man in jeans and a trench coat armed with an M16, stands in front of his simple blue cabin at the end of a dirt road. It's a beautiful snowy day. There's a doghouse behind the cabin but no sign of a dog. There's a fence around your yard, where someone, maybe you, has built a snowman. There's a stockpile of weapons hidden behind your house.

Out on the road is a moving truck, maybe implying the spree that awaits was not Plan A for how you would escape the town of Paradise. Unfortunately, your house is the farthest western point in the game. You cannot escape into the direction the truck was headed; you can only journey east into the gauntlet of violence that awaits. There are no choices in *Postal*.

As you look at the route designed for you, you notice the complete absence of soundtrack. You hear the occasional wail of a police siren, and indeed a police cruiser is parked out front as a guy who is likely a cop stands in wait. Otherwise, all is quiet. Then you emerge from the safety of your yard and the shooting begins.

There is no sense of spectacle or performance in how you mow down your neighbors and the local law enforcement. The only sounds are the guns and then the tormented wails of your victims as they twitch on the ground, bleeding out. Very quickly, this chorus of death rattles starts to loop and layer to such an extreme that it borders on a dance remix of tragedy.

I always expected *Postal* to be more of a lighthearted rampage. This is painful. And bleak. And not particularly fun.

The population of this first level is displayed in a menu above the game window. You must kill 90% of the "hostiles" in this area to move forward in your blood-stained journey. There is a total population here of 22, with eighteen of them labeled as hostile and only four as regular civilians.

After you get over the screams of the folks you've perforated, you'll notice that almost everyone in this world is armed to the teeth with high-ordnance weaponry. In the city of Paradise, a higher percentage of people own rocket launchers than have full-time employment. And they all seem to hate you.

You know what they say: It takes an army of good guys with rocket launchers to stop a bad guy with a rocket launcher. But am I the bad guy here? The good guy? Or are we all violent rivals in an amoral universe? We'll eventually get an answer but it won't be a satisfying one.

The first type of person you run across is a small army of identically dressed men who are most likely police officers. In full brown, they look like UPS drivers topped by winter caps with ear flaps. Very *Fargo*. They have pistols and shotguns that don't pose much of a threat to you, unless they mob you with sheer numbers. As the game's most basic baddie, it's a surprise when the first one takes nearly ten shots to bring down.

Every few shots, your rivals seem to take notice of the pain and let out a disturbingly real-sounding scream or exclaim, "I'm hit!" to no one in particular. Meanwhile, your avatar growls out *Terminator* B-roll quips like "Feel my wrath, dawg" or "Smells like chicken." You blast through other human beings who cry out in agony and you snicker aloud, "Sissy." It sounds as if the tracks are coming from two separate games: one pure camp and the other pure trauma.

Next, you encounter the much stronger bullet-sponge SWAT team members. They fire at you with shotguns and high-powered machine guns while circling you. They share the appearance of the basic police officers, except the SWAT guys are in blue instead of brown. Because of video game logic, this enemy type is harder to kill than the last. The presence of body armor only partially explains why they can take multiple point-blank shotgun blasts and keep dancing around you, unphased.

There are also a few paramilitary-looking dudes in green tank tops and baseball caps who clearly know as much about homeland defense as they do about fashion. They could be with the police, I guess, but they appear to be normal citizens in undershirts. They've come out on this winter day with unlimited molotov cocktails and grenades in their (presumably JNCO) pockets. Their placement is always specific, usually slightly off the beaten path of a level or hiding behind some bit of scenery: Everything is fine until suddenly you're on fire.

Finally, the casual militia guys have some buddies from work who show up in nice blue button-downs tucked into their khakis. These assholes have somehow requisitioned rocket launchers that can lock onto to your location and chase you anywhere you go until again you are on fire and maybe even a bit exploded. Questions arise about where everyone in this small town is buying heat-seeking, anti-aircraft technology. Is this all done under the guise of hunting? What would even be left of a deer?

Postal employs an *isometric viewpoint*, which is a visual style that hit its peak in the 80s and 90s: Imagine a bird's eye view and then bring it down to the side by 45 degrees. It's a trick that allowed 2D games to have the properties of a 3D world, and it makes everything sort of inadvertently cute. If you're an old enough gamer, picture the side view of block pyramids in the original *Q*Bert* or the lumpy grid courses of *Marble Madness*. Slightly less-old gamers might picture *SimCity 2000*, *Roller Coaster Tycoon*, *X-Com*, or *Super Mario RPG*. Baby gamers… I guess picture *League of Legends*, but with drawn backgrounds instead of actual 3D polygons? That's a game you play, right?

There's an inherently "gamer" draw to adopting God's perspective. The screen in *Postal*, for example, centers on your character but is also positioned at a distance where you can see at least a city block in all directions. You can watch your enemies scramble to retreat or double down on a new offensive against you before your character possibly could.

All of *Postal*'s humans are three-dimensional characters—not in motivation, but in action. As in other games of the era such as *Final Fantasy VII*, *Postal* drops blocky, 3D polygonal characters into a static 2D world. This choice makes the world's every object substantially nicer-looking than the people that inhabit it. It also grants every object impossible durability. With the exception of the exploding barrels, nothing in *Postal*'s world can be changed by your interaction. For example, firing a rocket launcher repeatedly at a house, a lamp post, or even a shrub will not result in that object changing at all. *Postal* is not here to let you destroy the world: It simply wants you to depopulate it with cruel, artless carnage.

You wind your way down a road you must have walked hundreds of times before, except today you're dodging homeowners with bombs and cubicle-chic terrorists, all of whom are seemingly deputized by the local police force.

For a man on a mass killing spree, the odds seem strangely stacked against you. Shouldn't you have an upper-hand here? The element of surprise? Perhaps you are not "going postal" after all, but are starring in *The Running Man*, and the entire world is working in harmony to murder you. If so, perhaps your only possible recourse is to kill.

Helping you along the way are small spinning boxes that replenish some of your health. In the woods or behind your neighbors' houses, you can find ammunition just hanging out. Sometimes there's also body armor that must have been discarded for being the wrong size or color. There are also rockets and bombs chillin' in random spots, which makes a lot of sense considering the sheer number of Paradise citizens who are explosive projectile hobbyists.

Postal is difficult, and it doesn't explain anything about its mechanics to you directly. For example, your basic firearm (and the only one with unlimited ammo) has a near infinite range and constant firing rate. Your shotgun, once you find ammo for it, is only effective at such close range that enemies cannot help but do serious damage to you. There's no animation to show that your bullets are doing damage to your targets, so you'll spend a lot of time wondering if you're missing your mark completely. In your first attempt to clear this area, you will die. Too many times. An embarrassing number of times.

You'll also acquire ammunition for guns you don't own yet, which is maddening. When you find perfectly good napalm in your rural neighborhood, but don't already have access to a suitable delivery system to rain fiery death upon your neighbors, it feels like a case of poor planning.

After learning to flank and spin around targets so you can take advantage of blind spots, you'll map out the level and the locations of the more deadly antagonists, and eventually work through a methodical cleansing of your neighborhood. This will be accompanied by the realization that you shouldn't use any of the "fun" guns or bombs, because they aren't nearly as effective as your infinite machine gun. There are all varieties of "mines," including proximity, timed, and shrapnel-filled, but in my entire playthrough I never successfully used any of them. Despite some truly terrible AI that sends your enemies running directly into your gun, it turns out none of them are going to stick around in the blast radius of a blinking device to see what might happen.

There is a sense from the very beginning of *Postal* that this massacre will be more work than fun. And it is. Over the course of twenty levels, you won't see much that you didn't already see in this opening level. There aren't, you know, bosses. All that changes besides the scenery will be the denser and more elaborate clusters of these basic enemy types while a few unarmed folks accidentally wander dumbly through the warzone.

For a broken man obsessed with revenge, your character's unhinged rampage is unfortunately pretty hinged. Like a census taker or a Very Wrong Santa Claus, you need to cross each individual off your list, but somehow the list is always expanding until it seems to envelop the entire world. In one reading, your bloodlust will never be quenched. In another, your blood-sponsibilities will never be fulfilled.

So the burden of figuring out what to do with these contradictions belongs to me, your faithful guide—a Virgil who unfortunately knows as little as you do. But by now you've already bought the book.

A CALL TO ADVENTURE

AFTER A FEW MONTHS OF being immersed in *Postal* culture, I'm near a breaking point. Not emotionally, but my patience for this game is running thin. It is jackassery. It is beneath me. Like a cultural prisoner, I've done my time and I'm looking to get out early on good behavior.

But I have so many questions. And if I don't ask them now, I never will.

So I track down Running With Scissors, the company behind the game, and send an email asking for an interview. The CEO, Vince Desi, replies quickly letting me know that he's leaving for the East Coast in a few days, but if I want to drive from Los Angeles to Arizona and meet them, I can do so the next day.

I get in my car and leave for Arizona. I'm going to spend the night in the home of a man I worry may be dangerous—or at least attention-starved, which is perhaps worse.

On the drive, my wife calls and asks, "What are you hoping will happen?" It's not a question I'd asked myself, and I do not have an immediate answer. I tell her I guess I'm hoping that there's something more to this game than what's on the surface. I'm hoping that Desi will be smarter than I expect. Will reveal that he was always in on the joke. Will explain how this least common denominator bullshit was a farce designed to exploit stupid people.

I've been looking at the company's Facebook page, where an active community still supports these games. I discovered that Vince Desi hosts a podcast about *Postal* and its sequels, and about the games industry in general. So I start my drive to Arizona by firing up the most recent episode.

In the first fifteen minutes, Desi explains that he's just heard about "some kind of accusations" against Casey Affleck. It's 2017, and the #MeToo movement is in full swing. Desi says he thinks Affleck is probably an asshole, but also claims that everyone in Hollywood is in some giant sex party—so who can call anyone out for abuse there? He jumps to the next topic, his belief that trans people are mentally ill, and then says he still does not understand why we have a Black History Month.

I turn off the podcast and call my wife back. "I'm not going to get what I wanted. No one here is smarter than I expect."

Postal entered my life with a sleepover gone wrong, and now it seems I'm about to drive eight more hours for another one.

GOIN' POSTAL

POSTAL'S WORKING TITLE DURING DEVELOPMENT was "Goin' Postal."

In the mid-90s, you heard the phrase everywhere. An image emerged in pop culture of US postal workers cracking under the pressure of their high-stress jobs and shooting up the post office.

There were news reports and op-eds, but also *Mad TV* sketches and late-night monologues. The 1995 film *Clueless* uses the term, though the cast did not themselves know what it meant. At the time, the trope was often played for laughs: an overworked postman in his little shorts who just couldn't hack a big boy job.

On an episode of *Seinfeld* from the era, Jerry asks his postal worker neighbor Newman why postal workers shoot people. "Because the mail never stops," Newman replies gravely. "It just keeps coming and coming and coming. There's never a let-up. It's relentless! Every day it piles up more and more and more, and you've got to get it out, but the more you get it out, the more it keeps coming in! And then the barcode reader breaks... and it's Publisher's Clearing House day!"

What I did not understand as a teenager at the time was how disconnected these sketches were from genuine postal worker violence.

According to a 1997 Associated Press article, the term "dates back to August 1986, when a postal worker in Edmond, Oklahoma, killed fifteen colleagues," though the article does not claim that people began using the term immediately after that killing. It would take until 1991 when two different postal shootings occurred in the same year (in Michigan and New Jersey) for the killings to be identified as a pattern. Actual printed evidence of the term "going postal" in popular media dates back to 1993 in Florida's *St. Petersburg Times*, most likely prompted by the story that follows.

On May 6, 1993 in Dearborn, Michigan, Lawrence Jasion killed one person, injured three, and took his own life—all at the post office where he worked and where he had just been passed over for a promotion. His main target in the shooting was Sandra Brandstatter, the woman who'd received the promotion instead of him. Brandstatter barely survived, but was shot in the face, head, and back. She had previously told police that she thought Jasion was a threat to her safety. Just before the shooting, they interviewed him and deemed him safe.

Across the country, mere hours later, Mark Richard Hilbun of Dana Point, California slit the throat of his mother (and her dog), and then executed a postal employee, shot another mailman, and wounded two others at an ATM. Hilburn was himself a former postal carrier who had lost his job in the postal service for stalking another postal employee.

May 6, 1993 was the day the entire concept of "goin' postal" coalesced under the same banner, albeit a somewhat arbitrary one. Two disturbed men who worked or had worked for the USPS revenged themselves against fellow postal workers on the same day. It's tragic, but it's hard to say whether the postal service itself is at the crux of the tragedy. It doesn't appear that the men were being pushed to unreasonable hours or that the USPS was in some way failing them. It's likely that it just sort of aligned that these guys were the guys who decided to kill some people. It could have happened in any profession.

But coincidence is not a great headline, and I've got to admit that linguistically "goin' postal" really slides off the tongue in a way that "goin' DMV" or "goin' air traffic controller" or "goin' vehicular insurance adjuster" does not.

As the phrase entered the mainstream vocabulary, the term loosened up. No longer was it specific to USPS employees, but was rather expanded to the idea of violence in any workplace, and particularly because of the workplace itself. "I'm about to go postal one of these days" became a sort of "God, is it Friday *yet*?" for the edgier Gen X set.

Soon enough, the phrase would come to mean even less. "'Pocahontas' is Going Postal" ran an article from July 19, 1995 in Rochester's *Democrat and Chronicle* describing how the Disney princess was getting a commemorative stamp. "Going Postal on Medicare" read a June 6, 1997 headline in the *Indiana Gazette* that has nothing to do with violence or even the USPS. At this point, the phrase was on par with the word "interesting"—depending on the context, it now meant whatever you wanted.

Maybe that's why the phrase has persisted even as post office killings have not. While the 1980s and 90s were full of high-profile cases, there were only a small number of incidents in the 2000s and 10s. This is despite the fact that in many ways being a postal worker has gotten much worse since the 90s. Strenuous routes. On-the-job injuries. Lower pay. Days "off" spent driving USPS trucks for Amazon.

One thing is for certain: We owe postal workers a big apology.

For me, researching this history has been one of those very modern wake-the-shit-up moments akin to the contemporary redemption of Marcia Clark, Lorena

Bobbitt, or Monica Lewinski after knowing them from my youth only as media punchlines. I have memories of grade school friends in hilarious costumes dressed as post office employees riddled with bullet holes. Today, the concept of "goin' postal" fits firmly in the category of 90s shit that we made into a joke instead of, y'know, dealing with.

And if we *need* an expression like this, let's find a more accurate one. On average, 100 people die in car crashes in the US every day. Goin'... Jeep? The CDC says excessive drinking has caused "one in ten deaths among working-age adults aged 20-64 years." Goin'... Smirnov? There is a mass shooting in the US nearly every day. Goin'... disaffected white man?

A PIZZA DATE

VINCE DESI REMINDS ME OF STAN LEE.

The creator of *Postal* and the CEO of Running With Scissors is an older dude and clearly a son of Brooklyn. He is a slight man with distinct features. His cheekbones carve through his face, and his eyes are entirely black. Picture an aging shark with a habitual cough.

Desi greets me, forgives me for being nearly two hours late, and insists we depart for a local pizza place on the double. It's nearly eight at night and I can't argue. A younger guy grabs a car and pulls it around in the driveway. Desi's assistant? I don't really make conversation with him. I have questions, but first I need to shove a glutinous cheesy mass into my idiot mouth. We don't talk on the ride. He doesn't ask about my drive and I don't ask about his horrendous politics. All is well.

We get out of the car in a mini mall parking lot. There's a small pizzeria that extends back in almost a straight line. I order the one item on the menu without marinara sauce.

We have a long pause. I think of myself as a pretty good interviewer, or at the very worst, a chill dude who can make conversation, but the silence from the car still covers us like a blanket. If they looked me up on Twitter Dot Com, they already learned what a feminist liberal nightmare I am, and they also know that I played their bad game. Pizza won't save us.

The assistant starts talking. He keeps talking. I really like him and he's a fun, cool, young dude being fun and cool and young, but I finally cut him off. "Who are you?" I ask. The implied question is, "Why are you talking?"

He gets it. "Mike Jaret-Schachter," he says.

Well, shit. I fucked up. I did a unit of bad journalism. Jaret-Schachter, better known as "Mike J," is the VP of Running With Scissors, second in command to Desi, and he's got the in-game cameos to prove it.

Now that I know his name, I recall the basics of his bio: When *Postal* came out, Desi's son was in high school with Mike J. When Mike learned what his friend's dad did for a living, he came to Desi and said he wanted to make video games, and Desi took him on to work on *Postal 2*, where he stayed on and kept moving up. So it's not great that I thought the co-owner of the company was our Alfred.

After we eat, the chef comes out to tell Desi and Mike J how much he loves them and how cool they are, and how he's shooting a reality show in Los Angeles. As they're paying, I grab a small bottle of whiskey from the CVS next door.

•

When we get back to Desi's place, I pour the liquor over ice in one of the only glasses in the kitchen. Desi and Mike claim the two best chairs. I pull up a shitty wooden Ikea chair, which buckles under my considerable weight. I put my iPhone on a footstool and begin recording.

Desi leans in. "You can ask me anything," he says. "But quote me without modifying it. You could be a good guy, and you seem like a good guy. But I've done a thousand interviews, including TV interviews." Mike J nods. "You don't have to like us," Desi continues, and then trails off. Desi's shark eyes connect with mine and I wonder if I look like the shark to him.

"When we picked the name Running With Scissors, people didn't like that," Desi says. "When I was growing up, my mom told me not to run with scissors. You know, it was supposed to be funny."

Without missing a beat, Desi continues: "People say *Postal* is violent. Fuck you." It's hard to argue with that.

"What about the marching band?" Desi says. "I love the marching band. Seven years ago we had an interviewer who laughed at the marching band. And then, when we were rolling on the interview, she shoved the microphone in my face and asked how dare I make a game like this?" Vince Desi's response to this professional journalist? "Honey, your twat's fucking soaking wet right now!"

For what will not be the final time tonight, Mike J leans forward and suggests that maybe Desi should not have said those words.

JUST LET ME BLOW UP A MARCHING BAND ALREADY

LEVEL 1 OF *POSTAL* ASKS, "What would it be like to go to war with your own neighborhood?" All the other levels of *Postal* ask, "What would it be like to... do more of the same, I guess?"

Level 2 takes place at a local truckstop. Emerging from a high-walled pass, you're ambushed by police hiding behind a parked vehicle. After clearing them out, you find yourself on the main road with a large truckstop on one side and a series of shops on the other side, including a delightful little donut place called "Honey Hole." Here, a dozen police officers, not originally numbered in the total count of hostiles for this level, spill out the front door of Honey Hole and the police station next to it. No one knows why the police station was built next to a highway truckstop.

The number of hostiles is nearly triple what you encountered on your home street, but this level is significantly easier to clear. That first level almost completely takes place in the open air, which leads to lots of potshots from unseen foes as you are repeatedly flanked. In "Truckstop," you quickly maneuver behind a line of buildings and meticulously pick off your attackers one at a time as they turn corners. Once in a while, a hostile futilely protests, "Stop shooting, you sick bastard—I'm already dead!" In *Postal*, even the cannon fodder gets the chance for a one-liner.

The only other gameplay twist introduced here are the blue barrels that explode when shot. It makes sense that the gas station would have giant vats of petroleum hanging around. What makes less sense is when they're arranged in a long winding row, built for the purpose of domino-effecting their explosions to take out a SWAT team.

Weirder still, there's a spinning box of general health out in the woods, boxed in by barrels, and the only dudes hanging around that spot keep lobbing grenades in random directions. I feel like this ends poorly for them, or all of us.

The next stop on your tour of terror is Level 3, "The Outskirts," which begins with an incredibly cheap shot: Three cops already shooting at you from close range. You dispatch them with the shotgun, for which you already have so much ammo that you can't possibly carry more. "Proudly made in the USA, baby," my avatar brags aloud—either about himself, or his guns, or the very concept of a mass shooting itself.

The big twist of this map is that there are many different elevation levels and small cliffs. As this is a painted, 2D world, figuring out the geography (and shooting range) of separate elevations is literally hit or miss. This is also the first time that the civilians are truly plentiful, and with the blocky art it becomes hard to tell when five dudes are all just chilling or if one of them is about to kill you.

Finally, *finally*, we arrive at Level 4, "Parade of Disasters."

If a single moment in *Postal* belongs in the greatest hits of gaming, it's either nothing at all or it's this scene right here.

We open on a wide city street. A building in center frame goes transparent, revealing your character on a side street. Hiding. Lying in wait. Unlike the other levels, music is playing: "The Stars and Stripes Forever."

Then, huh, it *just so happens* there's a parade coming this way. A marching band files down the center of the main street, entertaining a crowd that lines the sidewalks. The band is the only new character model you'll see for the rest of the game, and you will not see the band again, which is to say: Someone worked hard to create this moment. The band and their onlookers also collectively make up more humans than you have seen or will see on screen again. Folks, we've got ourselves a setpiece.

You inherently know what to do here. Maybe it's because you've seen a trailer for the game. Or maybe you're playing the game on Steam and you noticed the achievement. Maybe you've simply become fluent in the language of violent resolution from your first hour of *Postal*… and perhaps hundreds or thousands of hours of other, better gorefests. Or maybe you just hate the sound of marching band music. Whatever the reason, all roads lead to the same action.

You lob a molotov cocktail into the midst of the marching band.

Band members instantly burst into flames and run in every direction. Most make contact with other, non-inflamed individuals, and by proximity spread the death-curse of burning judgment throughout the city.

It's… pretty funny.

If you're not writing a book about *Postal*, I recommend you call it right there and put the game down forever. It's already shown off its only good trick, and there are, wow, fourteen levels left.

DRINK EVERY TIME
DESI LEADS WITH
SOMEONE'S ETHNICITY

I'M HAVING MY SECOND DRINK and I'm glad Vince Desi is not drinking too. He's already loosened up enough. I'm a bit jealous. I wish I could live my life this way. It's rare that you get to spend an extended period of time with someone who gives zero fucks about anything.

"I'm from Brooklyn," he says, riffing on his life. "I answered an ad in the *New York Times*. It said, 'Earn Big Bucks: 50K.' It was a sales job, but it was computer entry. But, you know, I'm also very creative. I was a painter. A creator. I produced *Rocky Horror Picture Show* off-Broadway. I was in the gay club business—or what you'd call raves. I'd get a person with the number one song on the radio to come lip-sync for us." I can picture everything he's saying. Desi seems like an offshoot of the Party Monster club kid scene—he's long aged out of it, but is still fun-loving, still free, still self-absorbed.

43

What's becoming clear is that Vince Desi does not want to be pardoned for being Vince Desi. He isn't looking to me to write a "nice" thing about him. He already likes himself plenty, and doesn't need positive press to bolster his self-image.

"A Jewish guy from Atari had a satellite office in New York that opened up," Desi says. "I jumped from accounts guy to a producer role and created Atari Labs. I'd just left Wall Street, but on my way out I did a few under-the-table deals for Atari. Then I was just [working for] Atari. I was basically, I dunno, an agent before that's how they were defined?" He looks and me and Mike J, and we nod in agreement.

"I put a programmer with an artist. This was Atari and Commodore. Then we got a deal with Children's Television Workshop. A guy I placed at Atari came back to me and we did all these titles with Disney and Sesame Street. We had so much work that the company moved out here to Arizona." I breathe. This was new to me: The guy behind *Postal* was the instigator of Sesame Street games.

He adjusts in his chair. He'd been a lawyer before all this and was afraid to give it up, so he kept making games while still protecting doctors from medical lawsuits. Then he was buying IPs for interactive development on the cheap because nobody gave a shit. It was like when George Lucas asked for merch rights on *Star Wars* and got them because no one thought merch rights would ever be a thing.

Desi detours to complain about that "bald-headed comedian fuck" he can't stand. Me and Mike J both guess as to who he means, and we're both wrong. "That Howie Jerk-Off Mandell. Total egomaniac motherfucker." Me and Mike J both go back to looking at each other.

Mike J is hot. He's an attractive, ripped bro that is either younger than me or my age. He's got a t-shirt that doesn't contain the years of gym time he's put in, but he's also so many decades distanced from Vince Desi that I keep pausing to try to solve the riddle of how this guy came to be co-owner of Running With Scissors. I have a lot of questions about Mike J.

"We made a *Bobby's World* game," Desi says, making it clear that his beef with Mandell was personal, "and that *Ghostbusters* game for Activision."

I lose it. *Ghostbusters* on the NES? A diehard fan of the movie, I grew up renting the game every weekend from our local Blockbuster despite kind of hating the game itself. Your team must venture around NYC busting ghost infestations, but you also need to tediously buy all your equipment to do so, even covering the gasoline costs of making it to your destinations. A comparable experience would be a *Blues Brothers* game where you need to pay the Catholic Church for every note you sing.

"We were doing good financially," Desi says of his company. "Then *Doom* came out and *Unreal* came out, and *Warcraft* came out. We needed our own game, and it had to be our IP."

So, *Postal*?

"Yes. *Postal*."

"So you have employees, and they're doing well, and getting a steady paycheck," I said. "But then you say, 'What if we killed a lot of people?' That was your plan for a new IP?" I know I'm being a dick, but I can also tell Desi doesn't care.

"There was a Chinese girl," Desi begins with his trademark light touch. "She wouldn't work on *Postal*. Fuckin' moral issue. We had a shirt company drop us because they found out who we were."

He's getting into a list of personal grudges and it's hard to follow. There's a Chinese woman and shirts. I indicate to Mike J that I need him to take over. He gets it.

"We had reviewers that told us that they liked our game," Mike says. "But editors told them they had to lessen their review scores. So the editor-in-chief of *Computer Review* said it was a 0% game. Their reviewer didn't think so, but his boss said zero. So we put that on the box for our re-release. The writer told us he wanted to give it a four outta ten. But then it was zero. That's when we started to have issues with the gaming press."

•

"I didn't find Postal to be dark," Vince Desi says about the game series where you hunt pedestrians with a shotgun for sport. "It's funny. I wrote dialogue and cutscenes for that kind of humor."

It's another tense stand-off in the room. This stand-off I understand better than the others. Earlier we'd been feeling out the general tone, but now it is a direct prod of "What do you think qualifies as humor?"

Desi explains that everyone was making their own game engine back then because no one had figured out licensing yet. In modern game design, it's fairly standard to pay someone else a fee to use their game making system, rather than losing years building a new one from the ground up. Early PC games were wildly varied because so many companies made their visions from a completely original foundation. The same was true of *Postal*.

"I asked [the programmers] how many people we could get on a screen at the same time," Desi says. "[And they told me] twenty. Maybe." He slams his hands down. "I want mass murder. I didn't want to kill one person and go hunting for the next, I wanted an entire marching band."

He laughs. "So they at least gave me a marching band."

THE MONOTONY
OF MURDER

In Paradise, there's only one clear path forward. From the moment we exit our house at the beginning of the game, a single dirt path points the way forward in a manner that suggests that this town exists not on a grid but on a jagged line.

At the bridge in Level 5, for example, the road crosses a river and ends in a parking lot, but then there's nothing moving forward from this point except for the entrance to a series of mines that serve as the next level. Why... why would anyone need a bridge here? Or a road? Where would these cars be going? Why was the only path to the mine through a trailer park? Could this whole thing have been avoided if we had just gone around the moving truck at the start of the game and headed west? Or like, stayed in the yard whispering our anxieties to our snowman like a normal, well-adjusted adult? "Only my weapon understands me," answers our character as he shoots down a human obstacle along the bridge.

No matter where you go, people have to die, and for some reason Paradise is a sprawling city-state with unending quadrants of population that simply cannot be sidestepped. Again, the entire world seems to be built on a linear pathway with no escape, so of course it makes sense that The Ghetto would lead to a Train Station, which would lead to a literal Military Industrial Complex.

Whatever you imagine in your head when you think of edgy 90s video game staples—these are the settings of the twelve levels remaining in the game. There are military bases, cities, trailer parks, a construction site, a farm, and even a carnival. But there will be no new enemies, no new characters, and no new gameplay, with one important exception: At some point ostriches start walking around. You can kill them, too.

With no further moments of chaotic blood-joy to build upon after the marching band, the biggest changes in game are simply background details and gags. The Air Force Base has a missile-firing helicopter you have to bring down, even though it's already on the ground. The aforementioned Ghetto level contains wig stores and payday loans, but also a desecrated church, and even the offices for Running With Scissors—where protesters with picket signs wait for you to fire on them and prove their concerns about the dangers of video game violence to be correct.

But it's not fun. None of it is. Every baddie, even on the easiest settings, is an absolute bullet sponge. Levels often trap a few characters in some far-off corner, forcing you to hunt them down long after the massacre portion of your experience has concluded. *Postal* becomes, oddly enough, a simulation of work. If you were to replace all of the bullets with mail and make this a game about needing to deliver ten pieces of mail to 100 random people in every map, this would be an accurate game about working for the postal service.

•

The game does have a story, though. Before each level, a dark image swirls queasily on screen, superimposed with a snippet of text, presumably from the main character's own head or perhaps from whatever demon is driving him. The first level begins with these ambiguous lines over a gaping mouth on a gray fleshscape:

The Earth is hungry. Its heart throbs and demands cleansing. The Earth is also thirsty.

And the second level kicks off with a dumb joke:

Blessed are the meek for they make easy targets.

But soon, we encounter more poetic jaunts:

Human trash spills from its containers as death rains down upon them, sweeping the streets in a cleansing cloudburst of blood...

I will don the eviscerated organs of my enemies as party hats, wear their shredded entrails as neckties, and oh, how I shall dance!

I am the celestial gardener, policing the planet of the stink weeds and poisons which leak out even through the cracks in the cold asphalt sidewalks of the City of Sin!

It's edgelord teen trash, but it seems to give us a window into exactly what this game is about: a deranged psychopath carrying out a holy mission only he can see.

And yet the game can't keep that straight, because the instruction manual *also* includes your character's notes on each level, ostensibly torn from the pages of your War Journal. They're bleak, but in a completely different way:

Moving to "Paradise" was a tragic mistake. People here are... sick. I hear gunshots, screams after dark. Now the phone calls, sayin' I'm being thrown outta this house. My house. Wearing Kevlar vest and carrying a sidearm at all times now…

Worst fears confirmed. Group of lunatics tried to invade my home. Must get to truckstop and Sheriff, see if anyone there can help me. Afraid only God can help me now…

Must face the possibility that I am only uninfected person in Paradise. Air Force must napalm entire town… ensure this madness doesn't contaminate rest of the country! Wait! I hear… music? Damn! It IS music! Better check this out…

Blood everywhere. Like a river, flowing around me, pulling me in its wake like a helpless child. It's all got to go now. The whole town. Prepare for… deconstruction!

These entries tell a completely different story about a man who sees the world going mad around him, or is at least interpreting it that way, who is on a noble mission to save Paradise from what could be a literal infection. Could it be that this has been a stealth zombie game all along? Am I a creep who thinks himself God's deliverer, or am I… God's deliverer?

These questions feel urgent until the next time I boot up the game. I shoot a cop dead, and my avatar sarcastically asks him, "Did that hurt?" and I must now contend with a third reading of the game: Whatever, bro! Just keep shooting that gun! At the heart of this game that didn't bother to crosscheck its in-game text with its manual text with its line delivery is a lazy, smirking nihilism.

I think we've found our answer.

FRINGE GROUPS
LOVE US

"YOU SPEND MONEY DEVELOPING. That's a developer's job," Vince Desi explains to me as if I am a child. "Publishers, however, are hard to come by. You can always find someone to test the thing, but releasing it—"

Desi sold the first *Postal* on concept, back when you could just elevator pitch a video game to your pal. With a million and a half dollars for marketing.

"We had a deal with Howard Stern," Desi says. I'm already laughing because Desi seems like he should have been Stern's childhood best friend; they're provocateurs who wake each morning to stir the shit.

Desi explains how Panasonic, the parent company of publisher Ripcord Games, bought ads on Stern's show. But when it came time for Stern to read the ads, he was baffled by this ridiculous, violent game and instead tore into it on the air. "Stern read the marketing on his radio show, line by line, and making fun of it," Desi says. "And Panasonic of America was [merely] the publisher of our game, [not the creator]. But Stern didn't know that, so he just kept making fun of Panasonic for making this murder game. [Panasonic] got cold feet. They backed out of publishing, gave us a few million dollars, and we weren't allowed to mention their name." It's ironic that Panasonic's cold feet came from Stern: His audience should have loved and supported the game for its First Amendment appeal alone.

Getting the rights back worked out for Desi. In its first week *Postal* sold nearly 80,000 units, making it one of the biggest opening week indie game hits of the 90s. Even 20,000 would have been a hit. But without the publisher involved, it was impossible to get more copies of the game on shelves in time. It literally sold out. And no further units were coming.

That's when Desi stands abruptly and walks into a different room. Most of the house is dark. In some of the rooms, I don't even see lightbulbs. The area that we are in is lit up, but even when I make a trip back to the kitchen to refill my drink, it's mostly illuminated by the fridge bulb. His art and belongings are in boxes that line the rooms. It's a large home that it looks like either someone is moving out of it, or into it, or that they can't/won't pay for too many lightbulbs right now.

I'm looking for Desi. He comes back in and hands me a trophy.

"This is an award I got from First Lady Barbara Bush, celebrating all the work I've done in childhood education."

We exchange a look. This award is real. I feel as though I'm entering a fugue state. I wish someone would take a picture of my face as I hold Vince Desi's Barbara Bush Award for a Real Good Job Helping Teach Kids.

Desi sits back down. "I used every possible means to promote us," Desi says. "I announced Running With Scissors before we even had the idea for a game. Then we announced *Postal*. Then we got sued over the name. Seven years later, we finally won that."

One of Desi's college friends became an intellectual property lawyer, which became helpful when the USPS sued Desi over the title. There wasn't an injunction during the lawsuit, so *Postal* was allowed to be released.

"We went down to our local post office, since we were using them to send out the game, and also deal with forms around the lawsuit," Desi laughs. "We gave all the employees *Postal* t-shirts and they loved 'em. They all got in trouble later."

I've been waiting to get into this. I think they can tell. I finally ask about their politics. With some certainty as to his answer, I ask Vince Desi if he's a libertarian.

"I'm a big fan of live and let live," Desi says. He explains how the game has always found support from the strangest of places. "When it first came out, there was a marching band called Brass Roots that supported us. A marching band, Brock." I get the joke. "There was a gay gamers group that loved and supported the game. Fringe groups tend to love us because we have condemnation for everyone equally."

Ah. The *South Park* defense.

"There was a Republican named ___," Desi tells me, "who everyone knew was gay. But he also passed anti-gay legislation. So when a Democratic friend of ours ran against him, we made a commercial where I said, 'Vote for Our Guy, That Other Guy Blows.' You get it? And that didn't make it to TV but radio stations covered it. They were shocked someone made it."

Desi's friend didn't win, an outcome Desi calls "retarded."

I tell Desi that I can agree with a solid one-third of how he operates, and the rest seems perplexing to me. I'd just written a travel piece for the site Thrillist about the best cities in each state for LGBTQ activities and safety. We're in Arizona, not too far from a small town named Bisbee, which was an abandoned mining town that is now a mostly gay community with an incredible art scene and a world-class Pride parade. I ask Desi if he's ever considered visiting Bisbee.

He tells me that Bisbee is where *Postal* is set. "We went there twenty years ago and shot a video, which we used as the basis for the levels." A game mostly about trailer parks and abandoned mines somehow makes more sense.

"There's an ostrich farm out there too." That explains the ostriches wandering about the town.

Later, this new information will make me daydream a conspiracy theory in which Postal Dude actually clears out all of the horrible violent people and their awful brass music to make Bisbee a secret gay paradise. But then we'd have to ignore so much else about the game: like how it ends.

THE ELEMENTARY
SCHOOL

THE FINAL LEVEL LOADS UP just like the previous seventeen. There's a dark quote with some nonsense on it followed by the name of the level. But instead of saying "The City" or "The Park" this simply says the following:

"The Elementary School."

The first time I make it to the level, I step away from my laptop. "Are you fucking serious?" I say to no one. It continues to load despite my protests.

Nothing I've seen so far gives any indication that the game has the vision or maturity or purpose to justify a level called "The Elementary School."

Ever since I began playing the game, it has been nudging, needling, even begging for my shock and outrage, and it has never delivered until this moment. Yeah, this got me. This got me good. Even twenty years after the game was released. Even after all the trash culture I've consumed. *How has no one ever mentioned this part?* I wonder. *How have I never seen it addressed in an interview? Does everyone quit long before?*

And then it finally starts. And sure enough, here is the playground of an elementary school, complete with swings, a teeter-totter, and a sandbox, drawn in the same style as all the other levels. Roughly twenty schoolchildren, all blond(e), run around, and then in runs the player character, right on cue. You may, like me, choose not to participate, but here it turns out that's not an option. It's a cutscene. Control has been taken away from me.

You hear the children laughing, and then you fire rockets into their midst. You throw grenades. The fire engulfs the playground, but the children remain unharmed. You hear screams, but no one is going down. You fire your machine gun in all directions. The bullets hit, but the children continue playing.

The children's laughter morphs into something more nightmarish as the screen begins to shake and tense horror music kicks in. Then a cut to black.

There's the image of a double-barred metal door and the sound of slamming, implying that you've been locked away.

Then, over the sounds of screaming that make the speech almost impossible to hear, a psychologist explains to an unknown audience what he makes of your situation:

Population pressure and the stress of modern life may cause an increase in violent tendencies. The urban environment is the incubator for all sorts of undesirable behaviors. However much this atrocity disgusts us, he may actually consider himself a hero. This is common among those who are referred to by the popular slang, going postal. In his tortured mind, he may feel he was battling against impossible odds. It is not unusual for some individuals to believe that the entire fate of the world rests in their palm. In the end, our subject displays all the classic symptoms of a paranoid delusional. We may never know exactly what set him off but, rest assured, we will have plenty of time to study him.

So ends this story, which finally firmly tips its hand away from the comparatively lighthearted "sane man against a zombie-ish hoard" tale of the manual and toward the narrative the title screens have been hinting at all along: a disturbed man's murder spree.

Finishing the game on that first playthrough, I was thinking a lot harder about this question: *What did I just sink all these hours into?*

If there's good news here, it's that RWS changed the ending when they had the chance. 2016's HD remake, *Postal: Redux* ends with a level called The End. You start in the lawn of a big church (uh-oh) whose front door is locked—thank God. You run through a field where you are surrounded by apparitions. There's a small funeral where a coffin is being lowered into the ground. You can shoot people at the funeral, but the bullets have no effect. As you realize the funeral is for you, the character falls to the ground and screams. Cut to the asylum.

It's a better ending to a much-improved game. *Redux* was made in a modern engine, and you can tell immediately that everything looks better, moves better, and plays better. It's also more firmly a game in a way the original is not. A new score-based arcade mode recreates each level of the game but increases the body count, new sillier levels add a greater sense of mischief and satire, and a new soundtrack of thumping rock music makes the screams of your victims sound a lot more cheerful. *Redux* is—I beg forgiveness—a fun game. And the new "your own funeral" ending keeps a horrifying school shooting from ruining the party.

It's possible that Desi and Mike J had no problems with the original ending and simply thought it'd be badass to have the main character attend his own funeral. But if I had to guess, I'd say that they looked at all of the real-life school shootings—the Columbines, the Sandy Hooks—that have occurred since the game's release, and conceded that their original ending was in poor taste. Maybe even Running With Scissors has its limits.

SEQUELITIS

To UNDERSTAND *POSTAL*, we must look at its sequel.

In 2003, Running With Scissors released *Postal 2*, the sequel to their outrage masterpiece. It's a better game, and was better-selling. *Postal 2* is the game a lot of people picture when they think of *Postal*. But it's also a game much clearer in its tone and intentions than the original.

The first *Postal* had a concept to explore and a "story" to tell, but the technology was limited and so was the developers' experience, resulting in a bizarrely disjointed game.

Postal 2 has little to do with the first game. Instead of a third-person isometric God view, *Postal 2* is a first-person shooter where you live in Postal Dude's head and see the world through his eyes. Instead of a level-based arcade shooter, *Postal 2* is an open-world game. Instead of presenting violence as something your character inflicts on the world, *Postal 2* takes you through the small, human moments of a mundane life until the violence comes for you. Instead of being the Grim Reaper, *Postal 2* makes you a stand-up comedian who maintains patience, even when faced with a world full of pricks out to destroy you. And with over four times the amount of the recorded dialogue, the lines that returning Postal Dude voice actor Rick Hunter delivers are far more jokey and meta this time around: "Video games don't kill people. I do."

Postal 2 is the opposite of *Postal 1* in so many ways that highlight the first game's deficiencies.

This is despite a slew of technical issues common to small studios who made the jump to 3D. Bodies twitch long after you've murdered them. Stray cats open doors. People randomly fire guns at you for sleights you haven't committed. But these bugs make the game that much more fun, and the game would be hurt if Running With Scissors ever cleaned it up.

The early 00s were a time when game technology was improving so rapidly that it was difficult for a company like RWS to keep up. The first game, with its painted backgrounds and repetitive levels, came out one year before Valve's *Half-Life*, which set the standard for first-person shooters… forever. *Postal 2* came out the year before *Half-Life 2*, which would raise the bar for shooters… forever… again. *Postal 2* wisely embraces its obsolescence, betting it could earn fans on verve instead of innovation.

The sequel opens with a long tracking shot through the city of Paradise, showing off a grossly cartoonish parody of post-9/11 America. Everyone is white trash, except the black people, who are twerking and shooting each other. The country is a powder keg about to explode, but also no one here is worth saving. That's when we get to Postal Dude, technically the same "hero" from the first game, who now lives out of a mobile home with his harpy wife who in this sequel is the game's true villain.

The plot revolves around a week of Postal Dude's life in Paradise and the banal errands he must run at his wife's request. However, none of these simple tasks can be completed without the violent intervention of protest groups with PC agendas. The opening mission takes you to Running With Scissors's office, where the Parents for Decency, a group protesting RWS's violent video games, become violent themselves, and you have to blast them down with machine guns. Then you can choose to execute the game's creators for being dicks.

Five minutes in, this feels like the game RWS wanted their first game to be. Fun, stupid, violent, and at everyone's shared expense.

Postal Dude, now clearly his own character with motivations separate from the player, maintains a cheery-if-Schwarzenegger-ish attitude towards a world that wants him dead. Unlike the first game, which rewarded you for clearing each level of nearly every living thing, the open world of Paradise introduces you as part of a community. Maybe that community is full of assholes, but there's little motivation to go on a shooting spree. Also, there's just a lot of people here. It's akin to the Grand Theft Auto series in that the player can choose to kill a bunch of people with little or no repercussions, but there's also an entire city of people who keep respawning, so to what end?

Because *Postal 2* has so much more going on than the killing, it's hard to even think of these two games as part of the same franchise. Postal Dude must get milk from the store and cash a paycheck and find a Christmas tree—low-stakes human tasks all around. Then rednecks kidnap you and take you to a rape dungeon straight out of *Pulp Fiction*, and the actual goddamned Taliban shows up and builds a nuclear reactor under the city. There's such grounding in Postal Dude's daily routine that the sudden escalation to the scale of global warfare absolutely broke me.

My biggest compliment to the game is that I couldn't stop laughing. Sometimes with *Postal 2*. Sometimes at it. Sometimes at myself for even playing it.

Postal 2 only built out from there. In 2004, the extra DLC content *Apocalypse Weekend* was released. Here, the apocalypse plays out over two more days in which Postal Dude is charged with executing zombies, dealing with his hallucinations of Gary Coleman monsters, and watching townsfolk torn asunder by infected cats.

Mike J is included in the game as a gigantic devil who is also the final boss, and there's a lot of genuinely impressive Silent Hill cross-dimensional stuff as Postal Dude's mental health declines—including walls made out of flesh. It's a worthwhile extension of the original storyline that tries some new tricks, throws in a few weapons and some uncouth jokes, and doesn't try too hard.

•

At Desi's house, I ask about *Postal 2*. I know I came here to talk about the first game, but Mike J wasn't there for any of *Postal*'s development, so he hasn't had a chance to weigh in yet. I want to know what he does, or what he did, and how it balances out the cult of personality that Vince Desi has achieved.

"We wanted an open world," Desi says, "but our engine…"

"We got beaten to shit [in the reviews] over that," Mike J says. "Over those load times."

The criticism was well earned. The game is set in a small town where every forty seconds or so, you'll encounter an invisible wall that triggers a long loading sequence for the next area. Especially when trying to travel long distances across the map, it becomes a technical nightmare.

"Before the game came out, there weren't a lot of open-world shooters," Mike J explains. "By the time we released [*Postal 2*], *Grand Theft Auto III* and *Half-Life* were both out."These were two of the best games of the decade. Not the kind of fight a *Postal* installment could win.

When I give Desi and Mike J shit for coming up against *Half-Life*, Mike J laughs and points at my face. "*We* released a third game," he shouts, referring to the infinite gestation cycle of the third Half-Life game, which never came out. "We released a third game," he repeats. "You write that down." I continue to not write anything down and let my iPhone keep recording.

Still, the success of *Postal 2* overseas led to new opportunities. "We went to Japan after *Postal 2*," one of them tells me. I ought to know this, but by now I've had several drinks and on the recording I'm just laughing.

"We were rock stars," Desi says. "We went to Moscow after Japan. A kid walked up and asked if I was Vince Desi. I said yes and he told me that this was so cool because he had decapitated me with a shovel. In the game."

"We were trapped on a plane with him," Mike J says, "and he wouldn't leave us alone, the entire flight." They'd inserted themselves into a game that was selling well, and the cameo had raised their profile as its creators.

I'm fascinated by the concept of rock-star game developers. It feels like a vestigial element of a bygone cultural era, like when Bret Easton Ellis was hosting MTV music video blocks.

"I did MTV in Russia at the Red Army Theater," Desi says. "It's the MTV Video Game awards. It's about as big as you can get. It's fucking crazy. I grabbed my crotch on stage and thanked them for Russian vodka and Russian pussy."

"It's not a joke that we sign thousands of autographs in Russia," Mike J says.

"We were signing pictures we'd taken with people five years earlier," Desi says. "We were at some whore house—this is my favorite Russian story. I said, 'You take the chink.' And she said, 'I'm from Kazakhstan.' We were surprised she spoke English. But she talked back."

It was as if the more I kept drinking, the more Desi felt emboldened to say whatever horrible thing he wanted.

•

The Postal games found a big audience in Russia—a stain on both our cultures—so it made sense for Running With Scissors to take the relationship to the next level.

After *Postal 2*, RWS partnered with a Russian developer to create a third title in the series, slated for release in 2007. Akella, the Russian studio, had a vast number of programmers dedicated to full-time production of what was to be the biggest and best Postal game yet, with better graphics and varied gameplay. The RWS team helped write scenarios, dialogue, and characters while their European partners built this state-of-the-art game.

Then Russia was hit by a financial collapse, and much of the Akella game studio bailed on the project—and on the game development world entirely. Programmers moved into fields like engineering and the financial sector, never to return to the world of offensive game jokes. The result was a delay of release from 2007 to 2011, and a game that wound up so broken most gamers couldn't even get it to run. Running With Scissors pulled the game from their own distribution within a matter of weeks and refunded everyone who'd bought a copy.

So by the time I bought a copy to write this book, I already knew what I was in for.

Postal III takes place after Paradise gets nuked at the end of the last game. Postal Dude and his dog set out cross-country in search of a new home. Instead, they wind up running out of gas near the town of Catharsis (jesus christ) and take on some entry level work in an effort to refill the tank and hit the road again. Instead, the Dude gets embedded in a series of apocalyptic and politically incorrect situations with high body counts.

The game exists in an over-the-shoulder third person perspective, always showing the view from just behind Postal Dude, and set in an open world that very much wants to be a Grand Theft Auto sandbox but has no ability to perform the basic technical requirements for walking around its world. Grotesque citizens deliver all their lines at the exact same time, weapons have almost no sense of hit detection, and any sense of humor that *Postal 2* may have developed is completely nuked here as the game forces you to endure endless cutscenes.

The delay from jokes pitched to jokes delivered in a five-year production back-up makes them so much worse. Postal Dude starts off getting a job at a porno shop run by Ron Jeremy where he makes minimum wage using a vacuum cleaner to suck up cum-filled kleenex that litters the store, and then uses those same jizz-rags to fight off an attack of Soccer Moms led by Sarah Palin.

From there, Postal Dude needs to clean up the town by helping local law enforcement in pursuit of cash for gas because petrol has become "retarded expensive." In one of the most confusing situations I've ever encountered in a game, Postal Dude regularly picks up giant quantities of gasoline that he can use to set people on fire. Not only does this gasoline fire rarely ever work to injure NPCs, but just one of these containers would negate the entire premise of the game. It's maddening that I can't pick up the gas I find at the beginning of the game, return to the mobile home, and be done with this.

Elsewhere, you'll need to protect movie director Uwe Boll from attack by nerds, stop "al-Qaeda Wetbacks" from crossing the border, and somehow navigate a morality scale for your actions that gives you the worst possible score when you accidentally injure authority figures. Because that's what people turn to a Postal game for: moral consequence.

This all culminates in cult leader Uncle Dave, Ron Jeremy, and Osama bin Laden teaming up to take you down. If you have gotten the "bad" moral ending for the game, it ends here, and you're mercifully free from the bonds of this timesuck. If you've kept your "good" score going, the game keeps going by having this Arizona town invaded by the Venezuelan army, and you square off against the ultimate big bad: Hugo Chavez in a tank.

After defeating Chavez, Postal Dude is elected President of the United States, and lives in front of the White House in his mobile home. It's a sadly prescient story, now that we must picture the discarded fast food wrappers that pile up daily in the Oval Office as Trump thuggishly leans on foreign leaders to take down his political rivals. Have mercy on us all.

•

And for many years, that seemed like the end of the Postal series. But then, in an unprecedented and ballsy move, they made a new DLC for *Postal 2*… in 2015, thirteen years after the original game came out.

The *Paradise Lost* DLC scrubs the world of the events in *Postal III* by returning to a place and a game engine from another time, to make a style of game that no longer exists and a political stance that never should have existed: The DLC is firmly pro-Gamergate, a 2014 "social movement" that claimed on its surface to petition for more rigorous ethical standards in video games journalism—which turned out to be a smokescreen for hateful online trolls to harass and threaten feminists.

Set again in the town of Paradise, the heart of *Postal 2*'s gameplay—the minutiae of "day to day life upset by frequent outbursts beyond your control"—somehow lives on even as various factions in the town violently vie for power. You're just living an ordinary life, but just by surviving you're constantly offending people and political groups. Along the way you have to do battle with actor Zack Ward (who played Postal Dude in the *Postal* movie), your formerly obese ex-wife who has lost the weight and become a trained ninja master, and bring down game developer Tim Schafer from Double Fine Games, who is holed up in a bank vault full of Kickstarter money while working on his game "Psycho-nuts." Schafer was likely targeted in part because he was one of the more publicly anti-Gamergate developers, having recently made fun of Gamergate trolls with a sock puppet at the Game Developer's Choice Awards.

In fact, instantly dated Gamergate references threaten to take over the entirety of the DLC. You can urinate on the grave of "Video Games Journalism." You can also meet Breitbart's former journalist cosplayer Milo Yiannopoulos at a gay bar where he assaults you with a dildo. Is this a free-for-all of jokes or is this trying to say something? It's clear the game sees itself as an Equal Opportunity Offender, spraying the landscape with "offense" and seeing what sticks.

There's no context for what to make of all this. It's pure reference comedy anarchy, and it's a total mess. The age group most likely to find the DLC transgressive is also too young to pine for some new *Postal 2* DLC. So why is RWS using their outdated *Postal 2* engine to appeal to the worst of gamers? As a lib, should I feel owned?

THE UWE CONDITION

"WE SAW BOLL'S FILM *RAMPAGE*. That was a lot closer to what we'd written."

We're on to the topic of the *Postal* movie now.

One day, a German teenager who claims to be the President of the German *Postal* Fan Club gets in touch with the Running With Scissors guys and says Uwe Boll should make a movie based on their game. The teenager says he can put Boll in touch with Vince Desi, somehow does so, and then disappears before he can even claim his agent fee for packaging this feature film. Boll tells them that he knew the kid because everyone in Germany (a small country of 82 million people) knows each other.

"I didn't know who Uwe Boll was, but Mike did," Desi says.

"Did you read—," I ask.

"The Something Awful article. Absolutely." Mike J knows what I'm talking about.

In a notorious 2005 article, writer Blair Erickson described the awful process of being hired to write a draft of Boll's *Alone in the Dark* movie, and being subject to a torrent of unhinged emails from Boll about future rewrites, complaining that among other issues:

> EITHER increasing numbers of people are getting kidnapped or killed by monsters, so that everything is threatened to go out of control and Edward has to stop the monsters – otherwise everything is lost in the end – OR Edward has to solve a specific case and stays on it – needs to go on an island (see ALONE IN THE DARK 4) or solve a murder. I was really angry, because I don't think, that you'd ignore so many things, that apply to story telling basics!

Having read the article, Mike J had an idea about the Faustian pact they'd be entering into. He told Desi to delete the email.

But then they watched some of his films and wondered if a B-movie icon like Boll might be perfect to adapt their schlocky game series. "I just wanted a movie based on *Postal*," Desi says. "It's campy shit. But I just wanted a movie. I mean, we all make garbage, but some people make better garbage. Can you imagine if Lloyd Kaufman made a *Postal* movie?"

Boll told the team they'd have creative control over the project, so there was an all-hands meeting at Running With Scissors where, over two weeks, the team hammered out a treatment. Then Boll abandoned their treatment almost entirely. "We wrote the welfare office scene that exists in the final film," Mike J tells me, "but it was not meant to be funny. At least, not like that."

Though Boll did not go with his script, Desi at least got a cameo in the movie. Boll apparently asked Mike J if he wanted to be in the movie as well, and he turned it down. "Fuck Uwe Boll," Mike explains. "He's a fucking maniac."

"One day on set," Mike continues, "there was a line-up of parents and they brought their kids, and then the kids were getting shot while the parents watched. In the script there was absolutely no context for this. Later we're in the office watching his cut and his producer tried to explain to Uwe that this wasn't funny."

Boll responded, "You're right, shooting kids is not funny. But. If we shoot a lot of them and do it to music, it *is* funny."

Boll does not care what anyone says to him, on any level, Mike and Desi explain. He's beyond taking advice. He's a doctor—of something—after all. Lead actor Zack Ward apparently later made his own cut of the film that Desi quite liked. But Desi is one of the only ones to have seen it, and getting eyes on the movie is what Desi and Mike see as the heart of the problem.

"It would have made money if anyone had seen it," Desi says. "Especially the college crowd. Universal was the distributor and our film came to sixteen theaters. Vivendi had the rights to this and *In the Name of the King* and they both were coming out at the same time. *King* got 2,000 screens. And everything, on down to DVD and streaming that was lined up for further distribution, was all contractual based on us having a wide release. Suddenly, it was all gone. It was all gone."

Desi rubs his temples. "Uwe also paid himself and credited himself for doing fifteen jobs," Mike says. "He was the boy grip on the movie."

This isn't his favorite part of our conversation. And no part of me blames him. It's hard to hand off your baby for another creator to adapt. It must be so much worse when that creator is famously shitty at what they do. Handing *Postal* off to a man best known for ruining film adaptations of video games, and then watching him do so, is a nightmare I would wish on no one. Even Vince Desi.

PART II

POSTAL: THE MOVIE

BY NATHAN RABIN

THE WORLD IS
MURDEROUSLY UNFAIR

IT IS GENERALLY NOT A positive reflection of your mental health or self-esteem when you find yourself relating, on a deep emotional level, to a man who has been widely, even universally derided as the worst person in the world at their job.

Yet by the time I spent several hours conversing with writer-director Uwe Boll via Skype from his home in Toronto, where he was cleaning up from an Easter egg hunt, pausing occasionally to clean out a waffle iron, exercise, or yell in German to some unseen soul, I started seeing a lot of myself in a filmmaker who has been mocked, insulted, and ridiculed, but never understood.

I identified with his world-weariness, with his disillusionment, with his sense of exhaustion, despair, and defeat. As a 43-year-old who increasingly finds it hard to make a living writing about pop culture 22 years into my career, I could relate all too powerfully to Boll's sense that there's not a place for him in the movie world anymore, if there ever was one in the first place.

Boll has never felt more confident in his abilities as a filmmaker or more despairing about his ability to continue to make movies in this environment. This is true even of the low-budget, self-financed, scruffy independent films like the bleak, mass shooting-themed Rampage trilogy, a series he's enormously and justifiably proud of, but that the world has ignored in a way it did not the early video game adaptations that made his name.

When the world was paying, if anything, way too much attention to him and his filmography, Boll made a series of notorious video game adaptations like *House of the Dead* (2003), *Alone in the Dark* (2005), *Bloodrayne* (2005), and *In the Name of the King* (2007), capitalizing on loopholes in German tax laws and starring screen giants and paycheck-seekers like Burt Reynolds, Ben Kingsley, and Jason Statham, that were derided as strong contenders for the unenviable title of Worst Movie Ever Made.

A few years ago Boll retired from filmmaking, just as I decided to retire from film criticism shortly after discovering that nobody was willing to pay me money to review motion pictures anymore after decades near the top of my field, first as the first head writer for the pop-culture juggernaut The A.V. Club and then as a staff writer for Pitchfork's short-lived, dearly loved film site The Dissolve.

Like Boll, I reinvented myself as an independent after the big sites and publishers were done with me partially in an attempt to secure some of that all-important independence and autonomy but also out of necessity. What do you do when the people who believed in you before don't believe in you anymore? You pave your own lane, or you get out of the business. At various points, Boll chose both strategies. As did I.

Yet filmmakers, like rappers and boxers, have a reputation for announcing retirements they have no intention of ever actually following through on. But listening to Boll, it felt like he was a world-weary survivor looking through the wreckage and debris of a film career he already sees in the past tense, as something that he did before, and not what he sees himself doing in the future.

Boll spent decades punching wildly in all directions—sometimes literally, in the case of his notorious 2006 boxing matches against haters—at film critics, fanboys, movie stars, and the Hollywood establishment, often doing sizable damage to his own career in the process. But now he just seemed tired of the whole business of film.

I feel the same way about film criticism. I chafe when someone describes me as a film critic because to me there's a concrete definition for film critic: someone who is paid money to review new movies. That was my life for eighteen years but it has not been for the past four. Oh sure, I write about film. I'm writing about film at this very moment! But I'm writing about film outside the context of film criticism, and that is at once exciting and a little terrifying.

The ferociously political, outspoken Boll has strong ideas about fair and unfair, right and wrong. And because he genuinely wants the world to be fair, it never stops hurting him that it's not fair, has never been fair, and will never be fair. I myself try to live with that brutal truth, some days more successfully than others.

That, on some level, is what *Postal* the video game and Boll's 2007 motion picture are about: life's unfairness. It's about shooting sprees as both a response to and a symptom of life's brutal, tragicomic unfairness on a micro and a macro scale.

In *Postal* the movie, the protagonist, known only as Postal Dude, suffers a gauntlet of life's small-scale indignities. The dude in front of him at the coffee shop takes forever to get to his order. Government bureaucrats prove a dispiritingly predictable combination of belligerent and lazy. In Boll's world, procuring a firearm and venting your frustrations via machine gun spray and mass murder has always seemed like a semi-reasonable response to the world's horrific unfairness.

Boll may have grown up with an overdeveloped sense of that unfairness. As you might imagine, he was not a terribly happy child. Blissful childhoods do not produce people like Uwe Boll—or me, for that matter. No, we are the products of damage and dysfunction, of anger and alienation. And of television. Forget Godard's children of Marx and Coca-Cola. Boll's movies are aimed unmistakably at vacant-eyed kids who stare at screens: the TV screen, the video game screen, and finally the laptop screen where his movies are disseminated (heaven knows there aren't a lot of folks out buying physical copies of Boll movies like *Blubberella* these days) and disparaged. Like me, he seems to live much of his life these days online, where he issues angry screeds and promotes his restaurant's appetizer specials via social media.

In *F*** You All: The Uwe Boll Story*, a mostly admiring 2018 documentary on Boll's life, films, and legend, Boll speaks glowingly of his kind mother and witheringly of his angry father, a championship handball player in his youth and a bitter man who did not hit his son but yelled at him every day. Boll's father did not read, and had no intellectual or artistic curiosity. He was at times cold and distant, and at others profane and corrosive.

In a 2017 *Vanity Fair* profile sympathetic to Boll yet still hostile towards his films, Boll elaborated on his distant relationship with his father: "My father was always yelling around. He taught me that I'm just a waste of time, told me I was a fucking loser, always cursed, and so on. I was brought up like this. It's normal for me in a way to talk like this. And it's tough for me to put that back. Or calm down, you know."

Boll's movies are consequently overflowing with anger, righteous and otherwise, toward corrupt authority. Boll is often described as a kind leader by his casts and crews, many of whom have worked with him over and over and over again. Actors in particular enjoyed how much room he gave them to try things and improvise.

But as a public figure and larger-than-life provocateur, Boll can be blunt and crass in self-sabotaging ways that have played havoc with his career and reputation. The provocation, the trolling, and the anger are largely ways of overcompensating for being a sensitive soul who was profoundly hurt by the world rejecting his movies.

As a child, Boll found escape at the cinema, where he fell in love with movies like *Godzilla* and *It's a Mad, Mad, Mad, Mad World*. As a schoolboy, he would happily act out the movies he'd seen for the benefit of classmates who couldn't go to the movies. He had one goal in life: to make movies. This passion would take him around the world and catapult him to a strange, unwanted form of infamy.

Boll's simmering adolescent rage had an unmistakable political component. Life was unfair because systems were bullshit and people could not be trusted. They were liars, hypocrites, and phonies. And when you are an angry teenager, everything looks like a system and consequently everything looks like bullshit.

Capitalism was a bullshit system, but Boll was equally cynical about other forms of government, reasoning, "All politics end the same: A few people have everything, and everyone else is fucked."

School was bullshit. Religion was bullshit, a lie people told themselves to feel better about the world's ugliness, unfairness, and brutality. Film school was bullshit, all theory, with no practical application. Of course Boll's fierce conviction that film school was bullshit, and the system for financing movies was bullshit, and that capitalism itself was bullshit, did not keep him from going to film school. Or from becoming a champion-level capitalist. Or from taking advantage of German tax loopholes more aggressively and famously than any other living filmmaker.

This rage powered Boll's first crack at making a real movie, 1992's *German Fried Movie*, an ultra low-budget, pitch-black exercise in guerrilla filmmaking whose transgressive naughtiness marks it as a spiritual sibling to *Postal.*

There exists within Boll a duality: He hates the capitalist game he wants so badly to win. When I worked in pop culture media, I used to recoil internally at all of the bullshit and compromise that came with my job.

But I didn't hate pop culture media as a whole *despite* working within that rigged, dirty system; I hated pop culture media *because* I worked within it. Interviewing and researching Boll, I saw the same tendency. He hated the system from the inside and the outside. All this misery was the price of getting to live out your childhood dreams.

Uwe Boll is at once a larger than life caricature, a towering Teutonic villain who delights in offending, and a sensitive human being deeply hurt by the contempt his work has received.

So while Boll has long raged against the world's unfairness and the innate failings of pretty much all systems, in the early part of his career Boll benefited tremendously from the world's unfairness.

Boll essentially discovered a magical money spigot that other hungry filmmakers either didn't know existed or didn't know how to use that allowed him to become a filmmaker on an international level while he was still learning his craft.

"The bizarre tax laws in Germany mean that any wealthy Germans who invest in a movie can write-off the production cost, delay paying their taxes, and generally reduce their tax burden," explains Stuart Wood in CinemaBlend. "The German investors in a movie only pay tax on any RETURNS the movie makes, their investment is 100% deductible, so the minute the movie makes a profit, said investor has to start paying tax. Plus the investors can actually borrow money to put towards investment and write that off too. Assuming you're a sharp enough businessman you have a potential goldmine."

So if the movie was profitable, you made money. And if it wasn't, it was all a write-off. It was like a magic trick. Using these financial maneuvers, Boll could make money for projects instantaneously appear, and then he was off traveling the globe to make the movies upon which his reputation is based.

Unfortunately for Boll—and it really is unfortunate—that reputation is for being the worst living filmmaker. That's no mean feat in a world where Tommy Wiseau and Neil Breen are both still alive.

To cite a typically vicious, personal pan, *Alone in the Dark* moved *The Austin Chronicle*'s Marc Savlov to write:

> There's a certain majesty to German director Boll's unmistakable style of filmmaking: a freedom from art, talent, skill of any formal kind, and the sheer pigheadedness to keep going at any cost and damn the straight-to-video market. That sort of single-minded, carefree attitude borders on the mystical if not the sociopathic. It's as if Boll, chasing his unicorn dream over the rainbow of anti-auteurism, has mastered

some deeply satisfying zen koan imparted to him by a wise man named Ed Wood.

Very early in his career, a mythology built up around Boll as a filmmaker of unique and appalling incompetence whose terribleness not only deserved but demanded to be mocked. Despite a seeming consensus among critics and fans that no one in the history of the universe was ever as bad at anything as Boll was at creating video games movies, Boll kept getting to make them. And with each new movie came a new round of glee and fury.

BBC writer Jamie Russell's review of *House of the Dead* ends,

> [*House of the Dead* is] so bad it could well go down in history as one of the worst zombie movies ever made. Which, in a genre that's given us oven-ready turkeys like *Plan 9 From Outer Space* and *Nudist Colony Of The Dead*, is really saying something. The only terrifying thing about it is the knowledge that Boll has already signed on to make three more videogame adaptations: *Alone In The Dark*, *BloodRayne*, and *Far Cry*. Somebody stop him. Please.

These reviews posited Boll as bigger than his movies in the worst possible way. A narrative seemingly sprung up overnight in which Boll was not just a bad filmmaker but the *worst* filmmaker, as a malevolent force who needed to be degraded into premature retirement.

Readers were amused and delighted with the vitriolic, over-the-top nature of these pithy eviscerations. Boll, most assuredly, was not. He did not appreciate that when he was profiled in the *New York Times* in May 2008, the headline was "Call Him the Worst Director (Then Duck)," or that the article began "Uwe Boll is often referred to as the worst filmmaker in the world."

There's only one word to describe Uwe Boll's feelings about receiving the apparently permanent title of World's Worst Filmmaker: unfair. Deeply, deeply unfair.

And while a lot of the internet was simply having fun at his expense, an amorphous but vocal group raged more earnestly that it was Boll's many opportunities that were unfair. Why did this guy get to make movies with Jason Statham and Ben Kingsley? Why not someone good who actually cared about the properties Boll was butchering? Boll in turn raged harder against video games, people who play video games, video game companies, and video game culture.

Boll was so apoplectic at the online roastings he received from respectable critics and amateur bloggers alike that he challenged his snarkiest and most vicious online detractors to boxing matches to prove, once and for all, his ultimate aesthetic value as a filmmaker. Or at least that Boll, who happened to be a skilled and experienced boxer, would be able to beat up some geeks. In September 2006, Boll won all five fights. Pummeling film writers with his fists astonishingly did nothing to improve Boll's standing with critics.

Now disillusioned with video games and video game movies, Boll told me that he considers *Postal* a huge step away from video game movies and towards the despairing, personal, and political cinema of the decade that followed.

Video games were like everything in the world: mostly garbage, but useful as a means to an end. By his own account, Boll has spent no more than 40 or 50 hours of his life playing video games. They just don't engage him.

Yet Boll had a revelation early in his career that would have a tremendous impact on his life's work: Low-budget genre movies based on established properties did a whole lot better commercially than low-budget genre movies not based on established properties. That might seem obvious, but for Boll it was nothing short of a career-maker.

Boll was in no place to acquire the rights to Transformers or The Lord of the Rings, but he was, and remains, sly and determined, savvy and calculating. So he was able to secure the rights to minor properties like Atari's H. P. Lovecraft-inspired survival horror game *Alone in the Dark*, even if that meant enraging *Alone in the Dark*'s fans to the point of apoplexy.

For *Alone in the Dark*, Boll wanted Jessica Alba to play the female lead, Aline Cedrac, a brilliant museum curator and archaeologist. Who he got was Tara Reid, the disgraced party girl and future fixture of the Sharknado movies, who ended up with the role largely because she shared an agent with *Alone in the Dark* star Christian Slater.

In Boll's mind, the miscasting of that role is the reason *Alone in the Dark* is derided. "Tara Reid made [*Alone in the Dark*] laughable" he bitterly insists. I'm not sure a universe where Jessica Alba was cast in the lead role in *Alone in the Dark* over Tara Reid would be any different than the one we currently inhabit. But when you're trying to pinpoint exactly why everything went wrong, it's good to have people to blame.

•

The universe had curious plans for Boll, his anger, and his complicated feelings about video games, capitalism, fanaticism, and Armageddon. As is often the case, the instrument for the universe's will is the curious entity known as the German *Postal* fan club.

As Boll explained to me—and Vince Desi explained to Brock—the German *Postal* fan club played a crucial role in connecting Boll with Running With Scissors: A member of the club not only clued Boll in to *Postal*'s existence but also encouraged him to hook up with Desi to procure the rights to the game.

It was the German *Postal* fan club that first saw the potential in an Uwe Boll/Vince Desi mind-meld. That knew that the most-hated film director among all gamers was the perfect man to bring the sick-joke world of *Postal*'s Paradise to life on the big screen.

So who exactly is the German *Postal* fan club? It seems possible to me that the entire fan club consists of a single strange, painfully intense man, who may or may not resemble Uwe Boll with a fake mustache. But we may never know.

The Postal video games (and more specifically *Postal 2*) trained their satirical aim at what bothered Boll about society, which is everything. *Postal* the movie reflects Boll's sensibility so purely that when I asked him what part of it represents his creative vision and which part represents Desi's, or the video game's, he answered instantly that the movie represents his creative vision one hundred percent.

Like Vladimir Nabokov's *Lolita*, Michelangelo Antonioni's *Zabriskie Point*, and Paul Hogan's *Crocodile Dundee in Los Angeles*, *Postal* represents a foreigner's take on American culture and the curious nature of the American people. But because this is an Uwe Boll production, it also involves Dave Foley's naked penis and Verne Troyer getting sexually assaulted by CGI monkeys.

Boll hoped that *Postal* would mark a turning point in his life and his career. He wanted it to be the movie that changed everything. He was going to make another video game adaptation, but one that actually spoke to him as a person and (secretly) as an artist. This would be his chance to show the world that he was not just some clown making dumb video game movies that meant nothing. No, he was going to be a smart clown making a dumb video game movie that meant something! To put things in Jack Horner *Boogie Nights* terms: This was one they were going to remember him for.

Postal wouldn't just be another movie. It'd be a pitch-black manifesto, a spit in the face of polite society from a man who unexpectedly found himself permanently miscast in the ferociously unwanted role of the world's worst filmmaker.

Postal would be Boll's revenge. The world owed him. It was only fair.

THE OPENING SCENE

MANY YEARS AGO, WHEN I had a job, benefits, and hope for the future, I reviewed *Postal* for my then-employers The A.V Club, an experience I wrote about later in the book *My Year of Flops*.

I wrote about the projectionist, who had screened the film for me and me alone, despite the enormity of the old-school film palace I saw it in, telling me abashedly, "The opening scene, you know, where the terrorists are arguing about the exact number of virgins they'll receive in paradise, it's almost, you know, kind of… funny."

The gentleman seemed profoundly surprised to find himself even on the verge of laughter watching a movie written and directed by Uwe Boll. And more than a little embarrassed. That's understandable. Society has conditioned us to not enjoy the work of people like Boll on anything other than an ironic level. Even Boll's own casts, crews, and collaborators tend to pay him back-handed compliments about how he's not as terrible as everyone says rather than praise him effusively.

I am here to tell you that there is absolutely nothing wrong about laughing both at, and with, *Postal*. There is no shame in it, just freedom: freedom from good taste, freedom from propriety, freedom from conventional wisdom, and freedom from the dictates of critics and cultural gatekeepers.

It's a trashy, vulgar kind of freedom, but freedom all the same, and in this world a thing like that is precious and rare, even in a riotous celebration of appalling taste like *Postal*.

The film opens in the sky as an airplane with a very specific and unfortunate destiny darts through the clouds. In the cockpit are a pair of terrorists who have already taken over as pilots. "We are at the doorstep of our martyrdom," one of them says with the serene certainty of true believers.

One terrorist delivers a monologue to the other about the unimaginable riches and pleasures that await them in paradise once they complete their mission: They will be greeted by Allah, the approval of their forefathers, and the eternal worship of "99 perfect virgins."

This concerns his co-conspirator. "I thought it was 100."

The other terrorist tells him that the exact number of perfect virgins doesn't matter. But the damage is done. In order to accomplish their mission, these men need the reassurance of absolute, objective truth, but the worried terrorist's questions stab a hole in that certainty.

All these men need to do is question a little and the complete fabric of their convictions begins to unravel.

Once the questions start, they don't stop: 99 perfect virgins are one thing, but maybe it's 75. "What if it's ten?" asks the worried terrorist: And what if it turns out there's only ten that must be shared between the two of them? That bumps the number of perfect virgins down to five apiece. And what about these virgins? "How long will five virgins last you?" he asks. "Maybe a month? They're not going to be virgins for long, right?" Eternity is a long time.

To calm his friend's panic, the other terrorist suggests they call "The Big Guy" to help them resolve their anxieties.

In the West's mind in 2007, Osama bin Laden was seen as a figure of scary, unknowable evil. In *Postal*, he is constantly being reminded of the many limits to his power. Without yet seeing him or even hearing his end of the conversation, our introduction to Osama bin Laden is very unimpressive. Bin Laden can't even promise his followers anything in the area of 100 perfect virgins. He explains to one of the frustrated skyjackers that it's a simple case of supply and demand, of "too many martyrs, not enough virgins to go around." In the upside-down world of *Postal*, the world's most notorious and feared terrorist is a harried yet bored middle manager who must walk back promises to his underlings.

Bin Laden can't go any higher than twenty guaranteed virgins. That's not enough virgins, so the two men make a decision with the potential to change the course of history. They decide to abandon their mission and take the plane to the Bahamas. Just then, however, a crowd of angry Americans burst into the cockpit and, in a tragically misguided attempt at heroism, steer the plane directly into the World Trade Center. Cue the opening credits.

In this revisionist take, the worst attack on the United States since Pearl Harbor was ultimately caused not by Islamic terror but by the oblivious enthusiasm of brave Americans doing what they thought was right.

Postal's opening is an inspired, even sublime sick joke that just happens to have the deaths of thousands of Americans as part of its punchline.

Yet the target of the sequence's humor is most assuredly not the people who died in 9/11, and certainly not the Americans who died trying to prevent it from happening. No, the satire in the opening scene is laser-targeted at the absurdity of trying to apply logic and reason to inherently fantastic concepts like religious martyrs being promised a healthy quota of untouched beauties as a reward for killing in God's name.

Boll isn't singling out Islamic dogma. No, *Postal* has contempt for all religious dogmas and all belief systems. "The one thing worth dying for is freedom of speech, freedom of thinking," Boll insists.

For Boll, the opening scene of *Postal* is about under-cutting the All-American Cult of the Victim, the notion that to die in a dramatic way in our culture is inherently heroic and not just a matter of bad luck, of being on the wrong plane on the wrong day.

As an artist he was understandably reluctant to cut his best scene, even if tonally it seemed to belong in a better, drier movie.

Unfortunately for Boll, granting himself the freedom to poke at the big cultural open wound that is the terrorist attacks of 9/11 might also have liberated him from any chance of getting a sizable theatrical release in a country that was still sensitive about the attacks six years later.

When I interviewed Dave Foley about the movie for *My Year of Flops* many years back, he expressed admiration for the scene along with a strong conviction that it should be cut. He told me, "I think that crashing a plane into the Twin Towers at the beginning hurt it. I said, 'Look, even though I think a lot of that scene is funny, a lot of the dialogue in that scene is funny, if you do that, you're never going to get on a screen in North America. So why do it?'"

Bear in mind, Foley's flaccid, not particularly impressive naked penis makes its film debut in *Postal*, so you certainly can't accuse Foley of being overly prudish.

Why did Boll include the scene if it had the potential to sabotage the film's theatrical release? Funny is invariably its own justification, but it goes beyond that. The warped, ugly beauty of *Postal* is that it is completely uncompromising, that it represents Boll at his most unhinged and free-swinging.

Boll wasn't just trying to make audiences laugh. He was here to provoke. To antagonize. To troll the world.

There's something appealingly perverse about the scene that caused the film, and the filmmakers, the most trouble—indeed a scene Boll and Foley could both point to as the reason the film did not receive a big theatrical release—also being the most acclaimed, sophisticated sequence in the entire film.

You have to be very funny and walk a very fine line if you're going to attempt to mine the bottomless psychic pain of the 9/11 attacks for yuks. Here, Boll walks that line with uncharacteristic deftness and sensitivity.

From an artistic and moral perspective, this scene needed to be in the film. It's essential. Yet there exists within Boll a penchant for self-sabotage I identify with all too strongly, a sense that there's no situation so charmed that it doesn't call for self-destruction.

The opening to *Postal* can be defended on aesthetic and comic grounds, but it also gave Boll something to blame if the movie failed. He could say, not without cause, that the funniest, smartest scene in his best and most personal film caused it to be rejected by distributors, theater owners, and theater chains. He wouldn't be entirely wrong, but that would only be part of the story, and one that's a lot more complicated than Boll makes it seem.

THE DIFFERENCE
BETWEEN A DUCK

With the flames of 9/11 still in the background, *Postal* announces its title on a battered and bruised license plate. And then, for that exquisitely Uwe Boll sense of literal overkill, the plate is shot repeatedly with bullets for good measure.

We then open in what Boll clearly envisions as the most American place on Earth, the ironically named Paradise, or more specifically, the Paradise Winds Trailer Park.

In *Postal*, Boll uses irony and satire as blunt yet effective weapons. It's a film of deliberate and intentional excess and hyperbole, a comic book hellscape of ugliness and casual brutality. It's the kind of movie where even the extras overact. If called upon to express pleasure, they all but hop up and down with giant, creepy "Black Hole Sun" smiles on their faces.

The ugliness of Paradise is physical as well as spiritual. The trailer where our emasculated hero Postal Dude (Zack

Ward) lives and suffers silently is a sad repository of broken dreams and bad taste.

For the central role of Postal Dude, an ordinary schmuck who is moved by the cruelty and randomness of fate to get a fuck-ton of guns and start blowing motherfuckers away, Boll got Zack Ward, a redheaded journeyman for whom *Postal* represented not just another paycheck but a once-in-a-lifetime opportunity to be a leading man. This was his shot, and he took full advantage of it.

Like Boll, Ward is a survivor. Ward managed to survive one of the most harrowing, toxic, and dangerous ordeals known to man—child stardom—to become a solidly employed character actor. Perhaps Ward survived because Ward's performance as Scut Farkus in the timeless 1983 holiday classic *A Christmas Story* was not one of the film's starring roles, just one of the most memorable. Ward was the bully, not the hero.

Since then, Ward has had an impressively consistent career as a working actor. In 2007 alone he starred in *Postal*, of course, but also found time to play "First Sergeant Donnelly" in *Transformers* for Boll's *bête noire* Michael Bay, to play Billy the Kid for a Western-themed direct-to-video BloodRayne sequel also directed by Boll, and to appear in the Kevin Kline sex trafficking drama *Trade*, episodes of *CSI* and *Girlfriends*, and a little-seen Mila Kunis/Jon Heder comedy called *Moving McAllister*.

If there is sweetness and light anywhere in *Postal*, it's largely the very Canadian Ward's doing. Ward, whose credits include the beloved Canuck miniseries *Anne of Green Gables* as the memorably monikered Moody Spurgeon, gives the character an innocence and vulnerability that have no place in this sick, corroded, decaying world. Postal Dude wants to do good. He wants to be good. In *Postal*, that comes off as not only suspicious but un-American.

•

When *Postal* was just barely released on May 23, 2008, a relatively new invention called the iPhone was changing the way we lived. But *Postal* takes place in a backwards world where wood paneling is still the rage, VHS tapes stack up in inelegant piles, and remote-controlled televisions are still considered a luxury. Not only does Postal Dude not possess a cellular telephone, when he calls Uncle Dave to beg for money to leave the living hell that is Paradise, he does so from a payphone.

A payphone turns the movie into an instant period piece, but it makes sense that a town as backwards as Paradise would still have its share of payphones. It's the kind of place that lingers anywhere from five to fifteen years behind the times.

The trailer park is where dreams go to die, but the marriage of our hapless protagonist and his obese wife died long ago. Dude's verbally abusive spouse is so big and so sedentary that she seems to be part of the trailer's infrastructure, a flesh-based component of a rotten little ecosystem as opposed to a human being who might someday leave the trailer.

For Dude, Hell is other people, beginning with his wife.

From the perspective of 2020, the comedy of *Postal* is all kinds of problematic. There is a lot of righteous, anti-authoritarian satire about the absurdity, violence, and greed of American society in *Postal*, but there's also a whole lot of misogyny and gay panic gags and fat-shaming and slut-shaming and nasty gratuitous violence and ugly stereotypes about Asian drivers.

Postal swings wildly, and some of that involves punching down, exploiting rather than commenting on some of the nastiness of American culture at its most unhinged.

Postal Dude begins the film still in thrall to the poisonous illusion that if he only follows the rules and does what society tells him to do, he will be rewarded with the solid middle-class existence long held up as the undeniable birthright of white heterosexual male Americans. He's gullible enough to imagine that an ordinary everyguy like him stands a chance in a rotten, rigged system, so he poignantly faces the day in the official uniform of hopeless strivers—black pants, dress shoes, a white short-sleeved button-up shirt, and a tragic little black tie.

We learn more about our hero at a job interview for an unknown position. Once upon a time he was a factory worker, that long-ago fixture of our country's industrial, pre-technological past, but then his factory was shut down, and nothing good seems to have happened since then.

The interview quickly takes a turn for the surreal. A woman with angry eyebrows informs Postal Dude that his responses to the kinds of questions that ostensibly have no wrong answers are in fact incorrect, before closing with the cryptic unfinished question, "What is the difference between a duck?"

It's American life in a nutshell: There are no right answers. You can't win. You lost the game before you even began.

When Dude senses the impossibility of his hiring, snaps, and yells at his prospective employers, they're impressed for the first time. The world is inherently angry-making: It's only when you erupt with murderous rage that people respect you.

In *Postal*, even when you win, you lose. The company is so impressed by Postal Dude's contempt for them that he's invited to sing the company fight song, a darkly comic ditty to the tune of "You're a Grand Old Flag" about the inexorable horror of working for this company, or any other. At the end of this confusing and weirdly invalidating experience, Postal Dude mutters his oft-employed catchphrase, "I hate this town."

•

Paradise is also home to a hippie sex cult, where the clock seems to have stopped sometime in the late 1960s and groovy space cadets illustrate their connection to nature by literally hugging trees. This is Uwe Boll, folks. Boll is not subtle.

The cult is run by Postal Dude's free-spirited Uncle Dave. Boll's first choice for the flashy, attention-grabbing role of a degenerate cult leader was *Hellboy* cult icon Ron Perlman, whom he'd previously cast in 2008's *In the Name of the King*. Perlman didn't just pass on the role. He told Boll he was offended by the script, which genuinely seemed to surprise Boll.

Instead, Boll got Dave Foley of *Kids in the Hall* and *NewsRadio* fame. Foley might not have been as big a name as Perlman, but he brings to the role a seemingly paradoxical half-assed total conviction befitting a guru who wants, and expects, his followers to worship him and do his bidding, but also isn't inclined to put a lot of time or energy into the gig when his limited time and energy can be reserved for the pursuit of hedonistic pleasure.

Uncle Dave runs the "Apocalypse Survival Center" at the Denomination Of Organic Monotheism (DOOM), a curious combination of Aquarian hedonistic commune and apocalyptic death cult. Dave understands that when enough goes wrong in your life, cults begin to make sense. I know that at various low points in my life I've contemplated both starting and joining a cult. Instead I opted to start a website and a podcast. The rewards are less intense, but so are the demands.

"Obviously you've come to the correct conclusion that the American dream is not a dream for you," Uncle Dave thunders to his flock. "In fact, it is a nightmare, a nightmare that soon will be engulfed in the ever-encompassing flames of God's damnation!"

Despite his words to the contrary, Uncle Dave seems to be living the American Dream. We cut from Dave proselytizing before his adoring flock to him lying on a bed with nubile followers in a state of undress. Like a lot of cults, Dave's seems to have become a sex cult quickly, almost as if that was its primary purpose all along.

Uncle Dave gets up from the pile of unclothed revelers, and roughly fourteen minutes into *Postal* the naked penis of Dave Foley makes its unexpected screen debut.

Why? The better question is, "Why not?"

It was reportedly Foley's idea to not do anything to cover up his naked penis when he gets out of bed, and

Boll loved it. It was a display of absolute commitment, of showing, in Boll's words, that "the actors are all 150 percent in." This brazen gesture was throwing down the gauntlet and establishing an "anything goes" spirit that distinguishes the movie. To the filmmaker, the cameo by Foley's penis set the tone of the film: casually debauched, gleefully irreverent, and delightfully excessive. The work of people deliberately going too far because they have nothing to lose.

To really drive this home, Foley then sits on the toilet and proceeds to defecate while reaching into a big bag of joints. This is not the kind of tasteful, restrained defecation you might see in a Merchant Ivory movie. No, this is gross, flatulent, repellent-even-by-*Postal* standards. The man doesn't even flush.

Uncle Dave's lazy Eden of hedonistic pleasure is shattered when Richard (Christopher Coppola, the black sheep of a Coppola dynasty that already includes Nicolas Cage), Dave's second-in-command, informs him that unless they pay the IRS the $1.3 million and 79 cents that they owe them, "everything is over: the weenie-whacking, the pantsless parties, taco Tuesdays. Everything."

Uncle Dave and DOOM desperately need a cash influx or Uncle Dave will go to jail and have to subsist on toilet wine and low-grade weed like an animal.

Postal surveys a nation that is spiritually tainted at its very core. Every institution is vicious and cruel. A black and white cop duo banter in classic post-*Pulp Fiction* style until the African-American cop becomes annoyed by a confused old Asian woman at a traffic stop, and shoots her in the face at close range with a shotgun. Later, the same cop fucks Postal Dude's wife while his partner enthusiastically films the action.

At a coffee shop tastefully called Grind Zero, acting legends Seymour Cassel and David Huddleston are truly brought low in the role of a pair of pervy old-timers. In the late 1960s and 1970s, Seymour Cassel was an essential part of John Cassavetes's repertory company, appearing in such seminal masterpieces of independent film as *Shadows*, *Faces*, and *Minnie & Moscowitz*. In the 1990s, Cassel lent a quiet dignity to the role of Max Fischer's barber dad in *Rushmore*. For his part, Huddleston had memorable roles in comedy classics like *Blazing Saddles* and *The Big Lebowski*. Here, Huddleston's character ogles a beautiful young woman and vows with disconcertingly avuncular glee, "One date with me and she'll look like she was hit with a mayonnaise truck!"

The welfare office is a soul-sucking nightmare of bureaucratic inefficiency even before an enraged aid-seeker whips out a gun and fires blindly, instigating a deadly and explosive gunfight that Postal Dude wanders through nonchalantly, like a Troma version of Buster Keaton.

Postal Dude picks up some lattes at a coffee shop and then pays a visit to his Uncle Dave, who appears to be the only good thing in Postal Dude's life. Dude becomes a different man around him. Less defeated, more at ease. We learn that Postal Dude wasn't always so beaten down by existence.

Uncle Dave and Postal Dude used to share a taste and genius for larceny, flimflammery, and the noble art of the con. Uncle Dave even gives Postal Dude credit for giving him the inspiration to pull off an ambitious long con like starting his own religion.

As these two simpatico souls reconnect, Postal Dude's personal backstory spills out artlessly: He and Uncle Dave were once partners in crime, but Postal Dude got busted and chose the infinitely soul-crushing path of the straight and narrow over a considerably more fun criminal one. Being around Uncle Dave reconnects Postal Dude to his wildness, to his true self, to the person he was before life crushed his spirit.

Uncle Dave and Postal Dude share a joint as they discuss the divergent paths they chose. In movies where men throw off the shackles of convention and reconnect with their younger, wilder selves, marijuana tends to play a central role, particularly in the earliest stages of spiritual renewal.

Smoking pot is just about the mildest, most relatable form of rebellion imaginable. For decades, it's been a technically illegal but also fundamentally harmless form of liberation. Pot may not be a gateway to other drugs, but in movies like *Postal* it's usually a gateway to other forms of rebellion.

Postal Dude barely has time to inhale before Uncle Dave is pitching him on being his partner in a mildly felonious endeavor. Uncle Dave articulates the film's philosophy when he tells his nephew, "Nobody plays by the rules, alright? You bend them or you break them. Anything less is slow death."

Postal Dude long ago chose the slow death route. But now he finds himself in a position to follow the dictates of that t-shirt in that Wham video and choose life. Uncle Dave is just the man to help him be his best worst self.

Postal Dude's evolution from sap to badass kicks into high gear when at a payphone he accidentally kills a belligerent con artist played by Michael Pare in self-defense. Though his first killing was justified, others will be less so.

But even at his most efficiently murderous, Postal Dude's body count can't compare to that of Bin Laden, who we're introduced to filming one of his trademark America-baiting videos before we pull out to reveal that the video is being made not in an actual cave but on a cave set on a big soundstage by an air-kissing, sycophantic, Hollywood-style director.

Larry Thomas, who plays bin Laden, is a quintessential Boll repertory player. He's famous, but in a spectacularly random fashion: He somehow managed to make an entire career out of appearing on *Seinfeld* once as the notorious "Soup Nazi." *Seinfeld* had been off the air for decades, but that hadn't done anything to dim the curious cult of the Soup Nazi. Here, he trades one tyrant for another.

Bin Laden is bummed because all anyone seems interested in is the virgins promised to martyrs. In *Postal*, there is no glory to jihad itself. It's just a means to an end, a way to get a grateful (and, to be honest, a little pimpish) God to hook you up with somewhere between nineteen and 100 virgins.

It turns out Osama wants the same thing as Uncle Dave: a lucrative shipment of Krotchy dolls, unnervingly testicular children's toys that look like a cross between Tickle Me Elmo and a diseased beige scrotum.

Thanks to an unfortunate accident involving a Chinese tanker, Krotchy dolls are scarce and the market for them enormous. Demand crazily exceeds supply, as with all those horny jihadists and much-sought-after perfect virgins, so these disgusting children's toys are fetching as much as $4,000 apiece online.

This leads us from one international villain to another, from a frustrated Osama bin Laden to a jubilant Dr. Uwe Boll. In the movie's fantastical world, Boll is both the filmmaker we all know and love, and the owner of Little Germany, a theme park that (according to popular American imagination) features everything that makes Germany *Germany*: bratwurst, beer steins, apple-cheeked young men in lederhosen playing polkas, and, of course, genocidal Nazis.

Postal was made over a decade ago, when Nazis were both figures of fun and fringe extremists like the conspiracy-minded political figure that future Academy Award winner J. K. Simmons plays here. We were still able to enjoy an innocent chuckle about Nazis instead of wondering to what extent the leader of the free world agrees with their beliefs.

Boll's rancid imagination runs wild with the Nazi theme park, which features such atrocities as a "Concentration Camp Playground" (a sign admonishes sun-seekers to "Turn right after gas chamber") and "Dr. Mengele's First Aid Station."

Boll is introduced in-film as a controversial director who made his fortune turning "video games into hit movies." I'm not sure the phrase "hit" has ever been applied to Boll's films outside this context—although many of them eventually turn a profit on home video, as evidenced by the many sequels to Boll's "flops." But his character is about to get shot in the dick, so I don't begrudge this sop to his ego.

To the mortification of the audience, a lederhosen-clad, beer-drinking Boll assures the crowd that the rumor that his movies are funded with Nazi gold is true. When Verne Troyer, the celebrity voice of the Krotchy dolls and the event's big VIP, shows up in Little Germany to greet his adoring public, he accepts his personal appearance fee from Boll in the golden teeth of dead Jewish children.

Troyer's appearance in the film is another piece of perfectly Boll casting. Like Larry Thomas the Soup Nazi, the late Troyer similarly knew the weird frustration of not being as famous as the character that brought him to the public's attention. In this case, Troyer rose to a curious fame as Mini-Me, Dr. Evil's diminutive doppelgänger in the Austin Powers sequels, and while good roles were few and far between in the ensuing years (when *The Love Guru* ranks as one of your most impressive late-period credits, something has gone awry), the concept of "Mini-Me" has stubbornly persisted in our cultural lexicon.

Boll has a definite type when it comes to casting. He's a consummate show-business survivor who gravitates towards other show-business survivors, men who were once primed for superstardom but took a wrong turn somewhere—or rather a series of wrong turns—and ended up in Bollsville. He doesn't just cast actors, he casts characters. He doesn't just cast characters, he casts fellow scoundrels.

These are men like Michael Pare, who received no less than three potentially star-making vehicles as a young man: 1982's *Eddie and the Cruisers*, and 1984's *Streets of Fire* and *The Philadelphia Experiment*. All attracted audiences over time, primarily through the everyday magic of home video. *Eddie and the Cruisers* and *The Philadelphia Experiment* even got sequels. Yet the cult nature of these star-making vehicles somehow never resulted in Pare being a star. Pare started out huge, then moved further and further to the fringes until he became something of a mascot for Boll, a familiar, grizzled face that has popped up in one Boll movie after another. Pare even worked as a ring announcer in Boll's boxing matches against his critics. In *Postal*, Pare is slyly cast as a belligerent bum convinced that even the film's sad-sack, put-upon loser protagonist enjoys a more enviable existence than he does.

But perhaps the *most* Uwe Boll casting is his casting of himself. Like all great leaders, he wasn't about to ask his collaborators to do anything that he himself would not do. For Boll, it was essential to depict himself as being just as disgusting, repellent, and cartoonishly evil as every other element of society. As not just a Nazi but also a pedophile, a Holocaust profiteer, and someone whose video game adaptations are not universally beloved.

This is driven home when an intense man dressed in a Krotchy costume takes off the costume's head and angrily/stiffly inquires, "Boll, I'm Vince Desi. What the hell did you do to my game *Postal*?"

"I don't know what you're talking about!" Boll insists of the movie we are watching at this very moment. "The movie is great!" This, friends, is what is known *and loved* as "postmodernism."

It is at this point that shit breaks loose. Pandemonium reigns. Boll shoots Desi as the fighting forces of DOOM, al-Qaeda, and corrupt cops turn the celebration into a bloodbath. Boll lovingly films the murders of innocent children in slow motion. He's absolutely heartless.

Uwe Boll, holding a gun in one hand, his other sheathed in a boxing glove (a winking reference to the boxing matches he'd challenged his critics to) gets shot in the dick and, echoing Postal Dude's frequent cry of "I hate this town," broods, "I hate video games."

Boll is admirably willing to suffer for his art. "It hurts to get shot in the dick," he assured me, even if you're not actually being shot with real bullets. Thankfully Boll's character did not bleed to death because if Boll had gotten around to making a sequel, he told me, his character would just come back minus a pair of testicles.

JUST LIKE LIVING AND
DYING IN PARADISE

Halfway through the film, Postal Dude has only killed one person, and that was by accident and in self-defense. That's not "going postal." That's having a shitty day. Who isn't at least tempted to kill at least one person a day? Particularly in this economy?

That changes after the Little Germany shootout. He spots a woman who was unpleasant to him at the welfare office and with a little-boy gleam in his eyes drives a truck into her. The speeding truck hits the woman, propelling her to her violent death with a cartoonish thud. At this point Postal Dude is a flat-out murderer. There's no going back.

When I interviewed Boll, he complained of the film's negative reviews, "A lot of reviewers talk about it like it's a trash movie but technically, it's super high-end! And it's expensive! There were like 50 speaking parts! There were big sets! And the CGI is top notch!"

I would never want to question the judgement of Dr. Boll but the CGI in *Postal* is not top notch. I wouldn't want it to be. I don't want polish and professionalism from Uwe Boll. I want craziness and passion and intensity. *Postal* is a better, stronger, weirder film for feeling in many ways homemade, like a ten-million-dollar home movie. In other words, I want Boll to be Boll and *Postal* to be *Postal*.

Boll lives with a lot of rage. In *Postal*, as well as the many films about mass shootings Boll would make following *Postal*—2013's *Assault on Wall Street* and the Rampage trilogy (which plays at times like a completely straight-faced, more overtly political version of *Postal*)—Boll is obsessed with the "X factor" that allows some people to push past the dictates of morality and commit the ultimate transgression: killing without remorse, purpose, or shame.

Then again, moral quandaries don't mean a whole lot after a certain point in *Postal*. We discover late in the film that Osama bin Laden's boys and the true believers of DOOM both have as their end games something approaching the end of the world. The terrorists want to use the Krotchy dolls to spread bird flu to the ignorant Western hordes. Uncle Dave's second-in-command Richard, meanwhile, turns out to be a true believer in Uncle Dave's Bible and consequently a believer in the apocalypse. He doesn't just want to use the Avian

Bird Flu to kill Americans: He wants to kill everybody, everywhere. He's all in.

It turns out that the DOOM compound has some features you don't see in many places. It has a windmill, for starters, as well as a massive bomb shelter Richard refers to as a "God shelter." Most impressively, and curiously, it has a room where ten thousand monkeys have been waiting to sexually violate a tiny entertainer as a prophecy has foretold.

Unfortunately for Troyer, he happens to be a tiny entertainer. And Boll doesn't just imply that Troyer is being fucked to death by animals: He makes that shit explicit. Thanks to the film's top-notch CGI, there's no doubt about what is happening to Troyer or how he feels about it: not good!

"All in all this has not been a pleasant day," Uncle Dave deadpans perfectly not long before he is murdered by Richard, also in fulfillment of the prophecy.

Postal is powered by comic rage. Boll's killing spree films to follow would remove comedy from the equation, leaving behind a white-hot core of pure anger. But in *Postal* Boll was still able to have fun with the poisonously dystopian nature of contemporary life. He was able to make it a joke. An exceedingly dark joke riddled with the corpses of children as some of its punchlines, but a joke all the same. A decade, countless mass killing sprees, and the election of Donald Trump later, things don't seem quite so funny.

Postal Dude is pushed and pushed and pushed. When his uncle is killed, he finally snaps and begins assembling an arsenal. The milquetoast everyman of the film's first act is replaced by a tongue-in-cheek badass in a peace symbol t-shirt on a mission to kill him some terrorists. He rips off the sleeve of his shirt to reveal an (ostensibly badass) anarchy tattoo. Postal Dude can only take so much before he goes postal. It is his destiny. It's right there in the name.

Postal Dude transforms into a trailer park version of Clint Eastwood or John Wayne. He's being hunted down in the streets of Paradise by a vengeance-crazed militia all out looking for what authorities describe as a rodent-looking dude in a peace t-shirt but he's also never felt so alive.

In a state of ecstatic fury, Postal Dude massacres the entire neighborhood watch with a machine gun in slow-motion. Boll's film is a delirious spoof of our culture's gun worship and gun fetishism, but Boll has a B-movie maker's pragmatic appreciation for the easy pleasures afforded by gunplay and epic shootouts.

Postal Dude teams up with Faith (Jackie Tohn), a tart-mouthed barista in the Ellen Page mold, and begins killing people who are trying to kill him, but also the occasional baby (by accident) and his wife (on purpose).

The trailer park becomes the setting for the next overcharged, corpse-riddled shootout between clashing forces ranging from Islamic terrorists to guys who just want to be able to continue fucking Postal Dude's wife without too much of a hassle.

Postal Dude gets everyone's attention by threatening to set off a big bomb and makes an impassioned speech that comes dangerously close to being sincere:

> What's wrong with you people? You're so busy trying to blow up the world in the name of God. News flash, fucktards: God doesn't need your help. He's God! And He, She, It, They gave you life and you're wasting it. Look around you, look. Look, goddamnit! See! We're not that different. Because we all come from the same family known as humanity. And what do families do? Do they fight? Sure, yeah. But they work it out. Because they love each other. And they know that they're stuck with each other, just like all of us are here, on this crazy big mud ball called Earth. So come on, people! Let's try to find some common ground. Not a hate thing, a happy thing. I think it's time to empty our hands of guns so we can fill our hands with hugs. If you want to waste this

precious gift we call life, I can't stop you. So go ahead. Shoot or hug.

Postal Dude is able to speak with moral authority despite being an irredeemable, murderous piece of shit because the sordid tabloid realm he inhabits is even worse than he is. It takes an ugly world to make Postal Dude look like a prophet of peace.

It's the Gospel of Uwe Boll reduced to its core: We can have a utopia if we put aside our differences and greed and anger and hatred and unite and become our best selves. Or we can be a bunch of crazy American motherfuckers and shoot each other.

The gun-wielding horde listens to Postal Dude's eloquent plea for understanding and non-violence. And, after giving his idealistic ideas a second or so of consideration, they begin shooting.

No one seems particularly interested in surviving the onslaught of bullets being dispensed by Postal Dude and his coffee house femme fatale accomplice with the notable exception of Osama bin Laden, who corrals a payphone to call his buddy George W. Bush to ask for help.

Just before pressing a button detonating the bomb in his trailer, setting off an explosion that will reduce Paradise to rubble and entrails, Postal Dude turns to his passenger and says, "I regret nothing." Then a rain of nuclear bombs from the United States and China rain down on a sick and immoral world, putting it out of its misery.

Osama bin Laden and George W. Bush complete this apocalyptic tableau by skipping hand in hand while an atomic bomb erupts in the distance. Just before the film ends, Osama quips, "Georgie, I think this could be the beginning of a beautiful friendship" with a distinctly Bogie inflection.

Boll began his most personal, most important, and best movie by blowing up the World Trade Center against the wishes of at least one of his stars and the dictates of good taste. He ended his assault on propriety by blowing up the world.

And, being the shameless B-movie carnival barker that he is, Boll still had the audacity to dream of a sequel. He even began a Kickstarter for it but pulled the plug when it grossed less than $30,000 out of a $500,000 goal.

More than a decade on, Boll is both proud of *Postal* and bitter about how it was received. He describes it glumly as a movie that everyone has seen and nobody has paid for, which is a little hyperbolic—but piracy undoubtedly hurt it.

The 2008 *New York Times* profile of Boll finds an optimistic Boll quixotically still hoping for a major 1,000 screen theatrical release for *Postal* even after receiving an email earlier that month from the chief buyer of the largest theater chain in the country reading, "While I have respected your past work, this film falls short of the type of product the Regal Theater Group would consider commercial."

I highly doubt that the chief buyer of the Regal Theater Group legitimately respected previous Boll efforts like *BloodRayne* and *Alone in the Dark*. Unfavorably comparing Boll's deeply personal new manifesto to the universally reviled likes of *House of the Dead* is crueler than rejecting it on its own merits.

This rejection gave Boll a noble explanation for the film's financial failure: The Man wouldn't give it a fair shot. The big shots were censoring him for political reasons, because he made fun of 9/11 and the War on Terrorism and W himself.

The weasel wording of the email subtly supports this interpretation. After all, he didn't overtly say that *Postal* was being rejected because it was bad. He was saying that Boll's *product*—product, not satire, not movie, not magnum opus—fell short of what it "would consider commercial." Not good or important or necessary: commercial. It's the kind of rejection that allows you to hold your head up high.

Boll doubled down on that line of defense in a statement he released around *Postal*'s intended release where he claimed, "Theatrical distributors are boycotting

'Postal' because of its political content. We were prepared to open on 1,500 screens all across America on May 23, 2008. Any multiplex in the U.S. should have space for us, but they're afraid."

"We have even tried to buy a few screens in New York and Los Angeles," he continued. "They won't let us even rent the theaters! I urge independent exhibitors to contact us and book *Postal*. Audiences have been expecting the film. I don't think exhibitors should censor what gets played in U.S. theaters."

Notice that Boll doesn't say that he was *booked* in 1,500 theaters but rather that they were *prepared* for a 1,500-theater release. There's a big difference.

I suspect that if distributors genuinely thought that they could make money off *Postal*, they would have booked it. Alas, *Postal* committed a crime far greater than making gleeful sport out of a recent tragedy: It was fundamentally non-commercial, a crazed provocation destined to play better among stoned cult movie audiences on home video than in theaters.

Satire has always been a hard sell cinematically. It's divisive and controversial and angry-making, when done right at least, but it also tends to die at the box-office. Think *Office Space* or *Idiocracy* or *Fight Club*. Satire fares better on television, which helps explain why three of the most commercially successful film satires of the last thirty years—*South Park: Bigger, Longer and Uncut*, *The Simpsons Movie*, and *Borat*—were all television spin-offs.

Despite Boll's high hopes for a big theatrical release and a healthy ad campaign, he ended up self-distributing *Postal* in a tiny fraction of the intended theaters. The theater where I saw *Postal* during its theatrical run seemed genuinely surprised by its existence; when I asked the woman who sold me my ticket how they came to be the only theater in Chicago showing the notorious video-game adaptation, she just shrugged.

Boll hoped that *Postal* would fare much better on home video, like his other movies, but piracy and the changing nature of post-theatrical distribution kept that from happening.

Boll had hoped that *Postal* and the more serious films that followed would change the way audiences and critics thought about him. But after *Postal*'s international release failed and the magical money spigot that funded his early, best-known films dried up, he found himself adrift. There wasn't a market for the kinds of movie he was making anymore.

So he quit. The almost suspiciously prolific dreamer and schemer who always seemed to be working on three movies at once—his last movie, his current movie, and his next movie—found himself losing his passion for the art and the business of film.

The directorial effort Boll insisted would be his last was, appropriately enough, another killing spree movie, 2016's *Rampage: President Down*, the strangely funereal and mournful conclusion to his Rampage trilogy. The Rampage movies are so unrelentingly dark and pessimistic that they all but co-sign the indiscriminate killing of its deeply disturbed but ferociously intelligent mass murdering protagonist as an understandable reaction to a world utterly beyond redemption. It's a sad, exhausted film from a filmmaker at an end.

Boll is proud that *Postal* has attracted a cult following among bad taste aficionados, but Boll remains an acquired taste few professional critics have acquired. In *F*** You: The Uwe Boll Story*, even the people who collaborated with Boll on *Postal* seem visibly, palpably embarrassed by their participation in his films and the extremes to which Boll would go for a laugh. Shawn Williamson, credited as *Postal*'s co-screenwriter, concedes that Boll shot the first draft of his *Postal* script. It feels like it: *Postal* has manic punk rock energy but also feels more than a little rushed and half-formed. *F*** You* depicts *Postal* as just another early Boll flop, not as a subversive creative breakthrough.

Postal did end up winning an award but it was not one Boll wanted. The filmmaker trying to make a statement about society and express himself as an artist was nominated for multiple Golden Raspberries, the ironic awards for the year's worst films.

In 2009 alone, Boll and his films were nominated for Golden Raspberries for Worst Picture (*In the Name of the King*), Worst Supporting Actor (himself), Worst Supporting Actor (Troyer), Worst Supporting Actress (Leelee Soibeski for *In the Name of the King*), Worst Screen Couple (Uwe Boll and "any actor, camera, or screenplay"), Worst Director (Boll) and finally, in addition to the six nominations for his films, the very first "Worst Career Achievement" for Boll in recognition for being "Germany's answer to Ed Wood." That is, the legendarily inept American director of low-budget genre films like *Plan 9 from Outer Space*.

The Ed Wood comparisons stalk Boll wherever he goes. At this point, he's probably more identified with Wood than Johnny Depp, who played him in 1994's *Ed Wood*.

Despite its ambition, audacity, and achievement, *Postal* was subject to the same withering reviews that greeted his other video game adaptations. Critics just weren't buying that Boll's movie was *supposed* to be funny this time, that laughter was its goal and not an inevitable accidental byproduct of his incompetence.

The *New York Daily News* gave it zero stars in a three-paragraph pan that begins, "Widely considered the world's worst filmmaker, Uwe Boll is now embracing his status by making movies designed to inspire outrage. Better to be disdained than ignored, right? Unfortunately, his newfound self-awareness has made his work entirely worthless. Where Boll's movies were once amusingly atrocious, *Postal* is so aggressively tasteless and knowingly idiotic, there's just no fun to be had" and closes with, of course, an Ed Wood comparison.

I was certainly on the high end of critical opinion when I gave it a mixed review at the time of its release for The A.V. Club, but my review was an apologist's surprised, abashed take rather than a full-throttled rave. "Only in Boll's upside-down world would a halfhearted assertion that his latest film isn't really all that terrible almost pass as a ringing endorsement," I wrote. "With *Postal*, Boll clearly set out to make history's most offensive, hateful movie. As is his custom, he failed spectacularly."

Boll has enough love for *Postal* to compensate for the world's hate and indifference. In a wildly self-aggrandizing interview with Destructoid, he boasted, "I think *Postal* is one of the best movies of the last ten years, and if it gets out there, you give it a shot and just see if you would see it, but it is not a good movie, it is a fucking great movie. I think it's the most important movie after September 11."

When he described his frustration at being once again named the worst of the worst by snarky assholes, Boll became freshly agitated. It wasn't fair! It was not true that he did not know where to put the camera. It was not true that he was incompetent. It was not true that his movies were unwatchable.

I could not convince Boll that these things did not matter, that the glib, dismissive judgments of the schadenfreude crowd will be forgotten while weird, imperfect, but ferociously alive personal statements like *Postal* will endure. *Indiana Jones and the Kingdom of the Crystal Skull*, a blockbuster from the world's most successful filmmaker, was released a day before *Postal* and went on to make nearly a billion dollars but today is fuzzily remembered as a bad mistake. Indiana Jones won the box-office war over *Postal* in a Harlem Globetrotters-like route, but history has been kinder to *Postal*, the little movie that couldn't.

It's the weirdos we remember, the Ed Woods and Tommy Wiseaus and Uwe Bolls, and not the acceptable, the mediocre, the forgettable. We revere and romanticize the best but we also remember the worst, or at least the colorful souls that are flamboyant, unforgettable, and distinctive enough to stand out from the pack.

In the *New York Times* profile a grateful Boll reflects, "As long as I'm able to make movies, I'm happy."

Despite his reputation as the worst filmmaker in the world Boll, got to make lots of movies. Many of his films are doomed to be forgotten, like 99 percent of all movies, but he's also made movies that attracted a lot of attention—usually for the wrong reasons but occasionally for the right ones.

That's a triumph in its own right. Boll may despise Ed Wood comparisons with every fiber of his being, but one thing Boll undeniably has in common with the *Plan 9 from Outer Space* auteur is that he's destined to be remembered long after "better" filmmakers have been forgotten.

PART III

POSTAL: THE MESS

BY BROCK WILBUR

ANGER MANAGEMENT

WELCOME BACK. ALL THIS TIME you've been exploring a bad-good movie, I've still been here in this living room with *Postal*'s creators, descending into madness.

"I consider Running With Scissors to be a club," Vince Desi explains. "There are active members, inactives, members in good standing… people we fired."

Desi and Mike J share stories of various employees they've had to let go over the years: a former EA exec that was always late, a guy who disappeared on a lie about his dead grandmother that ended when his grandmother (alive) called the company looking for him, and other boisterous tales of putting employees in their place. They used a Donald Trump style of firing that Desi feels has served them well.

"I'd greet you in the morning with all your stuff in a shoebox," Desi says. All three of us, in unison, quote the "get your shinebox" line from *Goodfellas*. It's a reminder that the three of us like a lot of the same things, even if we have much different takeaways. "That's why we have the policy now: Everyone who works with us starts as an intern. You volunteer. You show us that you want to do this. We don't have non-fans working here anymore."

The practice of running a studio based entirely on a worldwide system of modder interns who have to prove themselves for an unspecified amount of time in order to earn a paycheck seems unethical to me, but I get the feeling the modern ethics of employment don't interest Desi as much as the bottom line.

"That first Christmas after *Postal* came out," Desi explains, "we flew 40 people to Vegas. The team and our friends. We were whacked out on the plane on blow. We were at the Palms. It was crazy. Everyone brought their significant other. It was a big part of our budget. Most people wouldn't spend 50 grand on a Christmas party, but I think money is only important because you want to spend it. You can't take it with you. And these people worked so hard."

"We've got fifteen people right now. LA, Houston, North Carolina, Chicago, Canada, Ecuador, Germany, Italy, Ukraine, and the UK," Desi lists. "We have weekly, sometimes daily meetings. We had an office in Manchester for a while but we never even went."

Desi says that they were in Moscow when terrorists blew up the subway. He's become increasingly afraid of terrorist attacks over the years, and that influenced him into limiting his travel. I find it a bit twisted that the creator of mass murder games is now afraid of the violent world around him, but then again this fear may be at the heart of *Postal*'s existence in the first place: It's a dangerous world? Who can you really trust?

"We're always a few years behind because that's who we are." Desi is laying out what I assumed was probably a policy written on the Running With Scissors business card. "Technically, I mean, we're never competing. Our [*Postal II* DLC] *Paradise Lost* is twelve years behind the rest of the game world. But people never see all the work we put in. We make great stories and we promise that you're going to have fun, and we've never failed to deliver on that."

"Our games are crappy? No shit," Mike J adds. "Our budget was half a million. Our re-release of *Postal* was the 'Worst Game Ever Edition' and we owned that. Just like that, a player could now own the game on Steam for only one dollar. What else do you want, cocksmith?" Mike J has a mastery of both language and the invisible hand of the marketplace.

They both share stories about contemporaries of mine in the video game review world, who have admitted to them over the years that they never even played their games before writing reviews of them. I find this difficult to believe. Reviewers would never admit that to other reviewers, much less the people whose work they'd rebuked. Everything tonight comes with a grain of salt and a bit of dark liquor.

"That's where we get Milo and Gamergate from," Mike J says.

I straighten in my chair and feel a wave of defensive adrenaline kick in. It's time to push on this. I ask him to explain first, because I need to understand what internal logic lead them to support a hate movement.

"We came out as pro-Gamergate because we had journalists tell us they had to mark down our review scores," Mike J explains, "because we wouldn't buy advertising with their sites. They didn't want to do it but that's the business model that these corporations enforce. It's collusion."

"There's collusion in all of media," Desi inserts. "We're not pro-doxxing or harassing women. We were coming out in support of fixing journalism in games, and the media has fucked us in the past. That seemed fair to take on. The rest of this… the rest of what that became? None of that was okay."

Desi tells a story about a *Wall Street Journal* article that invented quotes about him, and the journalist behind it just claimed he ran out of time to talk to him. Desi felt violated. He reminds me to not fuck him over on this book.

"You've never had an anger problem, have you?" I ask.

"I'm chiller. I have a Zen book over there on a shelf." Desi does, indeed, have a book. I ask if it helps. Next to it, on the shelf, he points out a diploma. I thought it was a college diploma. It is for graduating from anger management. "We scanned that anger management certificate and put it in my office in *Postal 2*. I thought that was a nice touch. You probably just thought that was some [made-up] shit. It was fucking real."

Desi tells me he teaches anger management classes now. "Yeah, we even out. You work with what you've got. How could you spend your time being this negative? I'm not a negative person." I know he's not joking. That feels like the moment to end our night on.

As I thank Desi and Mike, I head towards the bedroom where I'd estimate there's an 80% chance there will be light bulbs. On the way, I pass the pile of art and unused frames, from where Desi pulled the award from Barbara Bush. There's a large frame next to it on the ground.

I do a quick double take, then circle back to where Desi is sitting. "Do you... Vince, do you have a framed copy of the Christian poem 'Footsteps in the Sand'?"

He does.

"It's a gift from my father," Desi says more softly than anything he's said all night. "He's 94. I believe we're all here for a short time. I cannot believe that I'm here to be miserable. I refuse to buy that." He adjusts in his chair. "This is not Hell. Every day is a new opportunity to be happy and to do new things, and those things should make you happy. Do what you can to make the world better and don't ever let yourself be a victim. No good comes from it."

Desi looks back at the poem, the one in which God whispers to a follower at the end of life,

> My precious child, I love you and will never leave you

> Never, ever, during your trials and testings.

> When you saw only one set of footprints,

> It was then that I carried you.

"I grew up in an 18-foot house," Desi says, as if further clarifying his position. "I slept on the fire escape."

I go to bed. I'm not sure if I missed the point of everything I came here to discuss. A man who is most famous for digitizing the fiery death of a marching band for the sake of laughs just reminded me that I can choose happiness.

I don't sleep that well.

I wake up early in the morning. I'm supposed to hang around for breakfast, but instead I shower, hop into my car, and head home. I later text Desi that I need to get home to a family get-together, which is true. But it's also true that I needed to get the fuck out of there.

We had our time together. I feel like what we shared was the best possible version of the three of us sharing a space. I repressed all my most deeply held political stances so we could be bros among bros. There was no reason to make eye contact again in the hungover light of day.

RETURN TO SENDER

HERE IS AN ENDPOINT. A little outro chapter.

I wanted to write about the game's cultural rele-
vance. How it intersects with the actual gun violence
we face every day. Many versions of this outro chapter
were written on the day of a mass shooting, wherein
the people at the highest level of power blamed the
vague concept of video games for these deaths, instead
of acknowledging that guns might, in some way, be
involved in gun deaths.

In the two years I've spent writing and rewriting,
what really stalled me was how tragedies kept happening.
The Harvest music festival in Vegas. The First Baptist
Church in Sutherland Springs. Marjory Stoneman
Douglas High School in Parkland. The Walmart in El
Paso. I kept thinking, *I've got to add something about
this one...* I insisted that the events of one singular day
would be worth wrapping up into a single moment that
could be projected across time and space as an example
of what we're up against. This was a fool's errand.

There have been a dozen times I've entered this document and have tried to tie-off the finale of this book by discussing the latest tragedy. But then comes the next: something so violent yet so integral that to not discuss it would feel like omitting part of the thesis. Tonight, there was a mass shooting in Texas. The shooter killed a postal worker and took her car for the rest of the journey. He killed seven more people, and shot a seventeen-month-old girl through the jaw. All because he'd just been let go from his job as a trucker. I looked up over my laptop screen, and saw a live-stream of a postal vehicle firing at innocent people.

There is no escape. I initially worried that the Postal Service might be full of dangerous people, but now I realize that yes, it is, and so is everywhere else. We're in constant danger. We are always at the behest of someone, somewhere, who has a gun and a chip on his shoulder.

Gabe, the lead editor of the Boss Fight Books series, finally had to intervene. "I encourage you to think of the nonstop run of mass shootings in America as a big phenomenon that you are approaching en masse and don't feel the pressure to follow up on or fold in every one of them," he wrote to me. "If it helps, picture someone reading this six years from now as opposed to today."

And holy shit, yes, unfortunately, yes. That was the advice I needed to finish the book. Because without acknowledging how fucking continuous this cycle of tragedy is, I had no endpoint. It's so bleak in a way that me of a few years ago wouldn't have accepted. But now here we are.

So how does *Postal* relate to our broken world? Ultimately, I think it's more symptom than cause.

Postal is a game about encouraging the absolute worst instincts of your reptile brain, in the service of the immediate dopamine rush that animated violence might unlock. It's a shooter among thousands, unique at the time only for its nastiness—for how it does away with any semblance of heroics, though at this point other games have improved on that trope too.

Honestly, even the developers are probably okay with that description. Those developers acknowledged from the outset that I would probably dunk on them for being assholes, and that was cool by them because assholedom was their entire brand.

Desi is, unabashedly, the height of the stereotypical Trump supporter: brash, impulsive, happy to speak on any topic—no matter how uninformed. And Mike J has been a Facebook friend since my visit. He regularly comments on my posts by asking "Where's my book, bitch?" Other friends inquire, "Who is this ass-hat?" and I reply, "Well, he's *my* ass-hat." I'm a Midwest kid. Most everyone in my family's orbit is not politically different from Desi and Mike.

Postal is a bad game made by guys with surface-level reactionary politics who expanded their game into a franchise with sequels and DLCs of wildly varying quality—with *Postal 4: No Regerts* apparently on its way. The reason these men keep getting asked about violent video games is that the mass media in general doesn't know shit about video games—they just remember a news cycle about some game in the 90s… what was it called? FedEx Man?

But it goes beyond ignorance. There's a concerted effort among the gun lobby to pin all these deaths on studios like Running With Scissors. NRA head Wayne LaPierre called video games "a callous, corrupt and corrupting shadow industry that sells, and sows violence against its own people."

Trump has invited people like Jack Thompson back into the White House. Everyone that had a good generic target in the 90s to blame shootings on? They're back. No one ever proved them as Forever Wrong, so now conservatives can grab them and make human shields of them once again. Is *Doom* the problem in 2020? Is *Postal* somehow the problem in 2020? Everyone Nancy Reagan once turned to for support in creating scapegoats for gun violence is now being invited back thirty years later to repeat the failures of yesteryear. And so much blood will spill because of it.

As I write this on September 1, 2019, the mayor of Odessa, Texas blamed a mass shooting on "video games."

Nothing expanding on that. No suggestion of proven life-saving policy changes such as thorough background checks, banning assault weapons or bump stocks, raising the buying age to 21, or requiring gun owners to go through training programs. Just the vague concept of video games. That was the entirety of his statement after 30+ people were injured and seven were killed, and he was asked how he might respond.

"Video games" as a concept has worked for years as a magic spell: Should politicians utter it, they assume that none of the blame for shootings will fall on their shoulders. Somehow. In 2020. The spell keeps working.

Postal is not the failure. We are the failure. This artifact from the mid-90s tauntingly reminds us of our cowardice. *Postal* succeeds in replicating the near-monotonous repetition of gun violence in our society, to the point where it is impossible to summon a positive or negative reaction to the game itself. It just looks a lot like the news.

In this way, *Postal* is ahead of its time. Desi and company inadvertently built a mirror for America that will outlive all of us. The man who won awards for educating children also predicted how so many of those same children would die. Running With Scissors set out to make edgelord schlock, and then the rest of the world made edgelord schlock out of reality.

ACKNOWLEDGMENTS

Brock would like to acknowledge Gabe and Michael from BFB for being incredible partners in this, as well as Nathan who is a better Best Man than he is a writer. He is also a very good writer. Tone is difficult to convey on the page. Thank you also to proofreaders Meghan Burklund, Matthew LeHew, Joseph M. Owens, to layout designers Christopher Moyer and Lori Colbeck, and to cover designer Cory Schmitz. There are some people that keep me functional by keeping me alive and without them this could not have happened: Alejandro, Brooke, Andrew, Tom, Marlis, Sue, Abby, Reb, Rowan, Kris, Zach, Zack, Sarah, Terence, Alec, Jordan, The Careys, Sydney, Woodward, Bernstein, Kimble, Athena, Christos, Laura, and prescription medications large and small. Vivian got thanked at the start of the book but she deserves to be mentioned here as well because oh wow am I a lot of work. Thank you honey for not asking too many questions when you saw me shooting up an elementary school on my laptop and I shouted, "It's for work." See? It was for work. I'm very normal and chill.

NOTES

To complete this book, Boss Fight editor Gabe Durham wrote or rewrote parts of unfinished sections, and then arranged the book from both authors' halves. Gabe is the sole author of the chapter "The Balls to Make a Game So Funny and Mean," added to the book for history and context.

Sleepover

Brock's dad was named a member of the *Salina Journal* Board of Contributing Editors on August 8, 1993 by the newspaper's editor, George B. Pyle ("A lucky 13 join Board of Contributing Editors"). His debut ran a few weeks later on August 26, 1993 as "Gramps butts heads with 'Beavis and Butt-Head.'" Through the rest of the 90s and into the 00s, his dozens of editorials tackled topics as diverse as cloning ("Multiplication without genetic variation," on March 10, 1997) and Beanie Babies ("Bean futures: An investment alternative," on May 3, 1998), but often enough, his love of his family. Of special note is the November 15, 1997 editorial "Salina public schools are falling between the cracks," in which he shares the byline with a young Brock Wilbur, then-editor of the Salina South Middle School *Cougar Special*.

The Balls to Make a Game So Funny and Mean

The *Wall Street Journal* article with the "from Miss Piggy to 'Kill the Pigs'" headline was Jon G. Auerbach's "Software Mutation: From Miss Piggy to 'Kill the Pigs'" from October 16, 1997.

News about the success of *Postal*'s demo version on Happy Puppy comes from Mitch Gilman's article "Tucson firm, video game violence in spotlight" from the September 15, 1997 issue of the *Arizona Daily Star*.

News of Jack Thompson's shift in focus to violent video games after the Heath High School shooting was eventually reported in articles such as James Prichard's "Parents of slain students to sue: Kentucky families blame film industry, computer game makers, Internet" published in the *San Francisco Examiner* on April 12, 1999. News of the suit's initial dismissal in April 2000 was reported in articles like Anne Thrower's "Report gives hope to Heath suit" published in the *Paducah Sun* on September 12, 2000. Thompson's disbarment was reported at Kotaku by Mike Fahey on September, 25, 2008 (https://bit.ly/2OBysBh).

Mitch Gilman's *Arizona Daily Star* article provided additional information on Walmart's banning of the game and Vince Desi's response, as well as on the boycott urged by the local American Postal Workers Union and Mo Merow's justification of it. The anonymous United States Postal Service representative who noted how the boycott backfired was quoted in John J. Fried's November 4, 1997 *Philadelphia*

Inquirer article "Violent computer game prompts postal ire: Rebukes help publicize the crude program, titled Postal! Sales are modest."

Running With Scissors celebrated their victory over the USPS's lawsuit in a June 25, 2003 press release entitled "'POSTAL' Video Game Victorious Over U.S. Postal Service; Running With Scissors Wins Case Brought by United States Postal Service."

Vince Desi reflected on the concerned calls from the FBI and the Treasury Department in Patrick Shaw's "The story of games studio Running with Scissors," published at PC World on July 9, 2010: https://bit.ly/2OIvWcx.

The "something for the whole (Manson) family" line comes from John Gaudiosi's review of the game in the "Screen Shots" column of the October 24, 1997 *Washington Post*.

For a comparison of *Postal* to *Falling Down*, see for instance Marc Saltzman's "Finally, a computer game worth gambling on" published in the *Toronto Star*, August 21, 1997.

Senator Joe Lieberman's "sick stuff" and "digital poison" quotes were reported widely, such as in Julian Duin's November 26, 1997 article "2 senators target video games' focus on violence, sex: Call arcades lenient on children's use" in *The Washington Times*. Running with Scissors took these insults as a badge of honor, quoting Liebrman in a press release issued that same day. The release, entitled "Santa Goes POSTAL Free Gift From POSTAL Game Developers" announced a "Santa patch" to introduce Christmas themed content into the game, with St. Nick "lobbing exploding presents from his bag of gifts." Also, they gushed, the "infamous ostriches from the original game version have been miraculously transformed into Rudolph's cousins."

The "sickeningly psychotic" advertising copy cooked up by Ripcord Games has persisted, accompanying online listings and gameography entries for *Postal*, such as this summary at VGChartz: https://bit.ly/37fJRwS.

Chris Dodd of London's *Sunday Times* reported on the initial international outcry against *Postal*'s violence in his October 5, 1997 article "Violent computer game sparks call for censorship." News of the alternative, censored version of *Postal* created for foreign audiences was reported in Australia's *Canberra Times* in the September 29, 1997 article "Postal Takes a Pasting." The final decision of the Office of Film and Literature Classification's final decision to "refuse classification" (that is, ban for release) for this "toned-down" *Postal* was reported by Phyllida Fitzgerald's article "Classifiers Clamp Down on 'Violence'" in the *Canberra Times* of November 3, 1997.

Mark East's review of *Postal*, "Postal Review: It's irreverent and gruesome to say the least, not to mention a little disturbing" was published by GameSpot on October 17, 1997 (https://bit.ly/39j8J8D). Michael L. House of AllGame gave *Postal* 3/5 stars in his review of the game, archived here: https://bit.ly/3bsQOxU. Game Revolution's review, titled "You lookin' at me? Are YOU lookin' at ME?", is here: https://bit.ly/2OFB412.

The generous *Washington Post* retrospective on *Postal* is Ariana Eunjung Cha's "Seeking New Twists on Violence," published March 16, 2005: https://wapo.st/2Sqh03y.

The Metacritic review was charliebeadles's March 12, 2008 posting, found here: https://bit.ly/39lA9dT.

Goin' Postal

Newman from *Seinfeld*'s quote comes from the season 4 episode "The Old Man," originally aired February 17, 1993.

The Associated Press's Arthur H. Rotstein reported on the history of the term "going postal" in "'Postal' game goes gory" in the September 2, 1997 *Arizona Republic* of Phoenix, AZ.

The growing pattern of postal shootings was identified by articles like Doron P. Levin's "Ex-Postal Worker Kills 3 and Wounds 6 in Michigan," published in the *New York Times* on November 15, 1991: https://nyti.ms/39xTt87.

The 1993 *St. Petersburg Times* article which documents "going postal" in usage is Karl Vick's "Violence at work tied to loss of esteem," published December 17, 1993.

Michelle Nicolosi and Robert Chow of the *Orange County Register* reported on the May 6, 1993 Dana Point violence, including the grim details of the canicide, as well as on the Dearborn shooting. Their story was run as "The job's murderous: Workers gripe of killer pace" in the *Philadelphia Daily News*, May 7, 1993, and in other newspapers with fewer puns. Another news piece by Larry Gerber of the Associated Press linking both the Michigan and California shootings ran nationally on the same day (see, for example, "At least 3 killed in Postal Service shootings" in the *Courier-Journal* of Louisville, Kentucky).

The "'Pocahontas' is going postal" article was written by Patti Singer for the July 19, 1995 issue of the *Democrat and Chronicle* of Rochester, New York.

"Going postal on Medicare" was the title the *Indiana Gazette* gave to a piece written by Scott Winokur of the *San Francisco Examiner* when they republished it on June 6, 1997. The original *Examiner* title from June 3 was "Medicare insurance shrinks for shrinks."

Although it doesn't promise an exhaustive chronology of postal shootings from the 1980s up through the present, Wikipedia does a fair job highlighting the major incidents in an article titled "List of postal killings" (https://bit. ly/37d8Cd9) and an the article on the phrase "Going postal" (https://bit.ly/2uzev79).

The Highway Traffic Safety Administration's National Center for Statistics and Analysis reported that "[t]here were 36,560 people killed in motor vehicle traffic crashes on U.S. roadways during 2018" in their "2018 Fatal Motor Vehicle Crashes: Overview" (report number DOT HS 812 826) published as an October 2019 installment of *Traffic Safety Facts: Research Note*: https://bit.ly/3bof3xm. The 2018 death toll averages out to 100 deaths per day.

The Center for Disease Control's "Alcohol Use and Your Health" reports on the "1 in 10 deaths" statistic: https://bit.ly/2HaCyvX.

The Uwe Condition

Blair Erickon's "notorious" article was "Behind the Scenes: Uwe Boll and Uwe Boll's Alone In the Dark," published on February 2, 2005 at Something Awful: https://bit.ly/2UKBfvX.

The World is Murderously Unfair

The 2008 documentary *F*** You All: The Uwe Boll Story* was directed by Sean Patrick Shaul.

The sympathetic-yet-hostile profile of Boll is Darryn King's "Game Over, Uwe Boll" published at Vanity Fair on March 27, 2017: https://bit.ly/39xTMzN.

Stuart Wood reports on Germany's tax laws in "Uwe Boll: Money For Nothing: The Awful Truth Behind the Worst Director in the World," published at CinemaBlend in 2006: https://bit.ly/2OFBUuI

Savlov Mark's review of Boll's *Alone in the Dark* was published on February 4, 2005 for the *Austin Chronicle*: https://bit.ly/3bviant.

Jamie Russell's review of *House of the Dead* for the BBC was published on October 25, 2004: https://bbc.in/2HbyoEc.

The *New York Times* profile of Uwe Boll is John Schwartz's "Call Uwe Boll the Worst Director (Then Duck)", published May 18, 2008: https://nyti.ms/2SejkvH.

The Opening Scene

Nathan's *My Year of Flops* was published by Scribner in 2010.

Just Like Living and Dying in Paradise

News of Boll cancelling his Kickstarter was reported by David Crookes in his "Postal 2 Strike: Uwe Boll Cancels Kickstarter Campaign to Bring Controversial Videogame Labeled 'Digital Poison' to the Big Screen" at the Independent on October 9, 2013: https://bit.ly/2OIxyTD. The Kickstarter campaign itself is here: https://bit.ly/38fVo0v.

Boll's claim that theaters were boycotting *Postal* for its politics was reported by Hunter Stephenson's "Uwe Boll's *Postal* Dismissed By US Theaters. Boll Whines and Whines," published at /Film on May 17, 2008: https://bit.ly/39ja5Af.

The *New York Daily News* zero-star review was written by Elizabeth Weitzman and published in the May 22, 2008 collection of reviews "Short takes: More movies out this week": https://bit.ly/2vn7V3D.

Nathan's mixed review of *Postal* was published at the A.V. Club on May 25, 2008: https://bit.ly/2OHK6dJ.

Boll's interview with Destructoid's Jim Sterling is "Exclusive interview, Uwe Boll, The Devil Himself," published July 5, 2007: https://bit.ly/2UDDgd6.

Return to Sender

Wayne LaPierre's condemnation of video games was reported widely, such as in Dan Zak's "NRA links violent media to mass shootings, but researchers are skeptical," published in the *Washington Post* on December 21, 2012: https://wapo.st/37dY2CXl.

The mass shooting in Odessa, Texas occurred on September 1, 2019. Mary Papenfuss reported on it at HuffPost that same day in "Odessa Mayor Blames Shootings on Evil People, Violent Video Games": https://bit.ly/31MeYPF.

SPECIAL THANKS

For making our fourth season of books possible, Boss Fight Books would like to thank Cathy Durham, Edwin Locke, Nancy Magnusson-Durham, Ken Durham, Yoan Sebdoun-Manny, Tom Kennedy, Guillaume Mouton, Peter Smith, Mark Kuchler, Corey Losey, David Litke, James Terry, Patrick King, Nicole Kline, Seth Henriksen, Devin J. Kelly, Eric W. Wei, John Simms, Daniel Greenberg, Jennifer Durham-Fowler, Neil Pearson, Maxwell Neely-Cohen, Todd Hansberger, Chris Furniss, Jamie Perez, Joe Murray, and Mitchel Labonté.

ALSO FROM
BOSS FIGHT BOOKS